Dying With Dignity

ALSO BY DEREK HUMPHRY

GENERAL
Because They're Black
Passports and Politics
Police Power and Black People
The Cricket Conspiracy
False Messiah

EUTHANASIA
Jean's Way
Let Me Die Before I Wake
The Right to Die: Understanding Euthanasia
Final Exit

Dying With Dignity

Understanding Euthanasia

by Derek Humphry

A Birch Lane Press Book
PUBLISHED BY CAROL PUBLISHING GROUP

A Birch Lane Press Book
Published by Carol Publishing Group
Birch Lane Press is a registered trademark of Carol Communications, Inc.

Editorial offices: 600 Madison Avenue, New York, N.Y. 10022
Sales & Distribution Offices: 120 Enterprise Avenue, Secaucus, N.J. 07094

In Canada: Canadian Manda Group, P.O. Box 920, Station U, Toronto, Ontario M8Z 5P9
Queries regarding rights and permissions should be addressed to Carol Publishing Group, 600 Madison Avenue, New York, N.Y. 10022

Carol Publishing Group books are available at special discounts for bulk purchases, for sales promotions, fund raising, or educational purposes. Special editions can be created to specifications. For details, contact: Special Sales Department, Carol Publishing Group, 120 Enterprise Avenue, Secaucus, N.J. 07094.

Manufactured in the United States of America

10 9 8 7 6 5 4 3 2 1

Library of Congress Cataloging-in-Publication Data

Humphry, Derek, 1930–
Dying with dignity : understanding euthanasia / by Derek Humphry.
p. cm.
"A Birch Lane Press book."
ISBN 1-55972-105-7 (cloth)
1. Euthanasia. I. Title.
R726.H83 1992 91-46786
179′.7—dc20 CIP

For Gretchen

The option of self-deliverance for the terminally ill person is the ultimate civil liberty.

—DEREK HUMPHRY

Contents

Contents

Dying With Dignity

Introduction

The 1990s is the decade when the issue of voluntary euthanasia for the terminally ill will be decided. Opinions are moving so powerfully for and against the right to choose to die that a decision cannot be far off.

Whereas the issue of a woman's right to an abortion has been in hot contention since the 1960s, it is my view that the length of the euthanasia debate will be shorter because the constituency is so much larger. Very few of us will be having an abortion, therefore we can safely theorize about the moral rights and wrongs of the procedure. Although we all try to deny it (some more vehemently than others), we know in our hearts that we are all going to die one day. Therefore the voluntary euthanasia issue is both pervasive and pressing.

In 1975 the "right to die" was not a problem in the public mind. The ugly side to the swift rise of modern medical technology suddenly hit us between the eyes the next year with the case of Karen Ann Quinlan, a young woman who was so severely brain damaged that her parents wanted the respirator disconnected, something the doctors would not do for fear of prosecution for taking a life. The court evidence about how it was now possible to keep alive people who had hitherto died, burst on an incredulous public. After a ruling that the respirator could be disconnected, there was a second shock. Miss Quinlan started to breathe on her own, but there was yet another piece of life support equipment in position: a feeding tube, which had not been the subject of the court case. With the aid of this gadget, Miss Quinlan lived for another nine years, dying naturally in 1985.

But was her "life" life as we know it, with awareness, feeling, response, and action? From all the published evidence, apparently it was not. It was a twilight world with the helpless young woman entombed in her own body. In the wake of the Quinlan experience—and in the many other well-publicized cases which followed—some people began making choices about their death based on their own estimation of the quality of their life. Living Wills—advance directives stating personal conditions about dying—became popular.

From 1976 onward there has been a debate about the

morality of disconnecting respirators and feeding tubes that keep thousands of people alive in a persistent vegetative state (or coma). Via numerous court cases across America, ending with that of Nancy Cruzan in 1990, the debate about the correctness of disconnecting life support equipment in cases of people in a hopeless coma appears to have been resolved. Now, in appropriate cases, with all-around permission, after careful consideration, the "plug" can be "pulled." From these developments we now have a new term: "a negotiated death."

Since 1978, when I first published *Jean's Way*, an account of how I helped my first wife take her life when terminal bone cancer became unbearable for her, I have argued that an honest and compassionate society must begin to address the problems of two types of euthanasia: *passive* (allowing a hopelessly ill person to die by refraining from treatment) and *active* (providing to a dying person who requests it the lethal drugs which can end their life). For people in the latter category there is no "plug" to pull, but they may be suffering greatly and desire a release by death. What the law calls "suicide" and what I call "self-deliverance" is the heart of the matter. And while suicide is not a crime, any active assistance in the act is felony.

A battle over the issue was waged in the state of Washington in the fall of 1991 when a voters' initiative reached the ballot, the first such test of public opinion in the world. Voters were asked to decide whether it should be lawful for a physician to assist the death of a terminally ill person. The initiative, which needed a majority to become law, was narrowly defeated in a vote of 54 percent to 46 percent. At the same time bills asking for lawful physician-assisted suicide for the dying were introduced into the legislatures of New Hampshire, Maine, Iowa and Michigan. Earlier in 1991 a euthanasia bill was introduced into the Oregon legislature, but it failed to get out of committee.

At the next presidential election (November 3, 1992) a similar question is due to be put to the voters of California, the most populous state in the Union, and the result will be considered a bellwether. Other attempts to change the law through the initiative process may follow in Florida and Oregon in 1994.

A majority of the public is seeking changes to the antiquated laws which forbid all forms of euthanasia. The proposed law in Washington State failed to pass because it lacked sufficient built-in safeguards to convince a majority of the voters that it would not be abused. Future legislation will contain extra precaution that take account of the public's wariness of the medical profession.

The essays in this book trace the steps toward the ultimate personal liberty: the right to die in the manner, at the time, and by the means that a competent adult wishes. In the name of compassion let the debate not go on for too long.

Derek Humphry
Eugene, Oregon
January, 1992

Chapter 1

The Great Debate of the 1990s

The astonishing sales success during 1991 of my book *Final Exit* surely said something about the way today's Americans view the prospect of dying: They are fearful of not being one of the lucky ones who drop dead or "pass away in their sleep," but instead ending up either as a "vegetable" or dying a painful or distressing death.

At last people are realizing that today we die differently from fifty years ago, and that it is wise to give the matter some forethought.

Final Exit was written as a "workshop manual" for the few (so I thought) who are deeply interested in voluntary euthanasia—the right to choose to die in a manner and by a means of one's own choosing.

The book's publisher, the Hemlock Society, is probably the smallest "small press" in North America (eight titles in ten years), and there was no advertising, no author tour, no hype.

Reviewers and columnists all studiously ignored the three hundred advance copies of the book sent to them. Unnoticed, the book quietly sold fifteen thousand copies in three months, until the *Wall Street Journal,* reported in its "Marketplace" column the existence of this controversial new book. Other media soon began to take notice. Within a week, all forty-one thousand copies had been sold.

So far, the book has sold more than half a million copies in the United States and Canada, and sales are still going strong. Publishers in nine other languages, including Chinese, have bought the translation rights, indicating worldwide concern about the "right to die."

The book has been recorded on audio cassette so that people on the move can listen to it on their Walkman. The Library of Congress has requested permission to transcribe *Final Exit* into Braile for blind readers. Two Hollywood film companies have telephoned asking for the movie rights! (Told they ought to read the book first, they have not called back.)

As the author and publisher, I guessed that the book would sell moderately well—perhaps forty-thousand copies over two years—because so many people had been asking me to write it. Undoubtedly, my previous three books over twelve years on the subject of euthanasia had helped build an audience for my writing.

But I would never in my wildest dreams have predicted a bestseller, at the top of the *New York Times* list in its category for eighteen weeks, and for two weeks first book overall in nonfiction in America according to the trade magazine *Publishers Weekly*.

As Hemlock's founder and executive director, I had noticed America's widespread disillusionment with the way we die, or else I would not be doing what I do, but I had certainly not reckoned with the extent to which people willingly take matters into their own hands, legally and medically.

Who Buys Final Exit?

Surveys show that most of the book's purchasers are middle-aged and elderly, and quite fit enough to walk to a bookstore and buy it. Bookstore managers report that the usual buyer was known to them already as a regular customer.

It was said that the book would seriously increase the rate of suicides among the despondent, but an increase has not materialized in the statistics or in any reports. Although there were initially some doubts expressed by bookstores about the wisdom of selling such a book, these dissipated an intelligent discussion spread nationally about the need for such a book.

In Canada, the more the book was condemned by

certain churches, the Right to Lifers, and some blinkered newspapers, the more the sales shot up. One Canadian wholesale book dealer insisted on buying ten thousand copies on a nonreturnable basis because the public demand was so great.

There Was Humor, Too

Bob Hope, Arsenio Hall, David Letterman, Jay Leno, and *Saturday Night Live* guests have all told jokes at the expense of the book and myself. The comedian who reads the send-up of the week's news on *Saturday Night Live* said: "This week Dr. Kevorkian's Mercitron machine killed itself, and *Final Exit* jumped from the top shelf of a large bookstore."

Cartoonists across the country lampooned *Final Exit*, suggesting that members of the Democratic Party and the Russian Communist Party needed to be its biggest readers! For me the wittiest cartoon was the one of the patient on a psychiatrist's couch who is asking his counselor: "Tell me doctor, why don't I want to read *Final Exit?*"

It has been said that once you have entered the language and lore of a country's humor and literature, you have truly arrived. The right to choose to die, voluntary euthanasia, has truly arrived. Above all, *Final Exit* has smashed the old taboo that you don't talk about the feasibility of suicide. It has demonstrated that the public knows there is a difference between emotional suicide and rational suicide; it is the latter that the book outlines, step by step, responsibly and lovingly.

At first, some suicide prevention groups expressed anger at my publication of this "how-to" book. There was even an anti–*Final Exit* street demonstration in New York City. However, anger against the book has diminished due to a heightened general interest in the subject, which can only be healthy.

Soon after the book's publication, I began to be deluged with invitations to speak at major academic and public conferences on suicide in order to elaborate on the two different kinds and to appear at fundraising efforts for help lines and hot lines. I am responding to the best of my ability.

At first, workers in some suicide prevention centers were shocked that people were calling them up and saying they were depressed and were reading *Final Exit.* Then it dawned on the workers that it was a good thing that people were calling them—after all, that's what suicide prevention centers are for! *Final Exit* repeatedly pleads for depressed people to seek support and treatment.

Why Are People Reading This Book?

Let's not fool ourselves: many people are fascinated to read about how others have ended or would end their own lives. I have noticed a widespread curiosity about the subject which many people are reluctant to admit to—and now *Final Exit* demonstrates the extent of that fascination.

Several times when the publicity about the book was at its height, I was invited into radio or television stations and the producer or host would say, "Mr. Humphry, we have some doubts about the wisdom of putting you on to talk about any form of suicide."

On those occasions I would quickly respond, "Oh, that's all right, I don't want to embarrass you. Let's drop it and I'll go home now." In a flash their squeamishness would disappear and they would make up their minds to proceed with the show.

But the deeper reasons for America's desire to read this unusual book on how to kill oneself appear to be:

- Dread of spending one's last days hooked up to equipment, bells, and buzzers while breathing and feeding through tubes, either through natural orifices or surgical slits.
- Reluctance to risk putting the family through long and draining court battles similar to those courageously fought by Mr. and Mrs. Joe Cruzan for four years to get their daughter, Nancy, disconnected from life supports after a serious automobile accident.
- Disillusionment with the effectiveness of the Living Will, which is only a *request* to die. A doctor may ignore it. (I still recommend its completion as an expression of one's wishes.)

• A fear of losing control of one's life and body as medical procedures gradually take over during an illness.

• A horror of spending one's final years in a nursing home with an unacceptable quality of life. When visiting an elderly aunt recently in her nursing home, I heard another inmate groan, "Why has God allowed this to happen to me?" My aunt, ninety, commented, "Old age can be a terrible thing."

• Dread that the physician attending one in the final days is poorly trained in pain control, or has qualms about administering large doses of drugs because they will either cause addiction or indirectly bring about death. (This category of doctor is diminishing, thankfully.)

• Concern that one may be among the 10 percent of dying people whose terminal pain cannot be managed without their being made zombies by massive doses of narcotics. (Although marvelous strides have been made in pain control through the sophisticated use of drugs in the past twenty years, it is arrogant for anybody to claim that *all* pain is capable of being controlled.)

• Suspicion that the medical profession has become purely business and cares more about income than alleviating suffering. (After lawyers, physicians are the least-admired people.)

• Fear that one's health insurance will run out just

when one needs it most. (This is particularly likely with AIDS patients.)

• Finally, and probably most important, the desire to be in charge of one's life and the dying process. Personal autonomy is extremely precious to many people, especially those who have considerable achievements behind them, and consider that they have led a full and useful life.

What must be done to dispel or reduce these justifiable fears?

One. Physicians must receive better training, not only in pain control but in ethics and law, and learn how to develop a more compassionate relationship with their patients. Too often the public sees the doctor as purely a body technician and part of a team of strangers who are administering mysterious treatments.

Two. The medical profession must learn to drop its ridiculous claim that doctors are purely healers. Everybody, even a doctor, dies eventually! Aid-in-dying in appropriate cases and on a voluntary basis must become part of good medicine.

Three. The laws and rules about the responsibilities of hospital management and health professionals toward patients must be clarified. Physicians have to be better trained in how to practice "informed consent"—the legal right of the patient to know and understand what his options are. The new Patient Self-Determination

Act, which took effect throughout the United States on December 1, 1991, will help by obligating all health-care facilities—at the risk of losing federal funding—to inform all incoming patients of their right to refuse treatment.

Four. The public must insist that the Living Will laws now in existence in forty-four states be fully respected. Similarly, the Durable Power of Attorney for Health Care must be adhered to. (This latter document is legally enforceable.)

Five. More members of the public must sign these advance declarations expressing their various wishes on how to be treated during dying. An estimated 20 percent of Americans have signed these declarations. While the number of signers is rising, it is still ridiculously low.

Six. All states must pass the Death With Dignity Act so that physicians who are willing to assist the suicide of a dying patient who requests it can be free from prosecution. Groups in the state of California are currently engaged in voter initiatives (a sort of referendum) to pass this law because legislators, already bruised by the abortion rumpus, will not risk getting engaged in further controversy.

I do not regard the success of *Final Exit* as a reason for gloom about the contemporary state of mankind, even though some people have seen it that way. I see it more as a patients' revolt against the inadequacies of modern medicine, together with a desire by the public to talk more openly about ways of death. If the book's message and sales figures serve only to shatter the fusty intractibility of the American Medical Association and push medical schools and doctors generally into positive action to help the dying, then it will have been worthwhile for that alone.

Most of all, I think the popularity of *Final Exit* is making that most American of statements: "If you won't help me, than I'll handle it myself."

Chapter 2

Why Euthanasia Lost in Washington State

Defeated by a narrow margin at the polls in Washington state on November 5, the pro-euthanasia movement is asking itself why it lost when most public opinion tests, including those in Washington, say that sixty-five percent of Americans approve of euthanasia.

Why did the support which predicted victory slip away at the last minute? With signatures already being gathered in California for a similar law reforming initiative the results of the inquest are critical.

Initiative 119 in Washington sought approval for lawful physician aid-in-dying for the terminally ill. The request would have to be in writing and two doctors would be required to determine that the patient was likely to die within six months.

In the Seattle area many people blame the defeat on

the furor over Dr. Jack Kevorkian helping to end the lives of two women in Michigan two weeks earlier. The specter of maverick doctors "on call" to assist the suicides of people whether or not they are judged terminally ill was potently raised.

Kevorkian—the loose cannon of the euthanasia movement, not affiliated with any group—in my view, may have marginally affected the result but not significantly. My extensive contact with people interested in euthanasia shows that a great many Americans admire Dr. Kevorkian's basic principles—the right to choose to die—even if they have doubts about his methods and strategy.

The two chief reasons for the Washington defeat, in my view, were:

1. **Semantics.** The language of the campaigners was to the language of the media and the public as apples are to oranges. "Aid-in-dying"—as the campaigners called it—can mean anything from a physician's lethal injection all the way to holding hands with the dying patient and saying "I love you."

They avoided the words "suicide" and "euthanasia" as though they were obscenities. The media, ranging from the tabloids to the learned academic journals, along with the public, used the real words with relish.

2. **Safeguards.** The Washington campaigners made the tactical mistake of painting their law with a broad

brush, intending to sit down with the medical and legal professions after victory to hammer out the detailed guidelines under which euthanasia would be carried out.

But the public did not want euthanasia laws on the books without built-in safeguards—a sign of the general distrust of the medical and legal professions.

The *Journal of the American Medical Association* of November 27, 1991, states, "Medicine got lucky in Washington's historic vote this month to reject physician-assisted suicide for the terminally ill." According to Peter McGough, MD, state medical association spokesman against 119, "This time we were very lucky, but this is not the end of the debate; it's only the beginning."

The forty-six percent vote is seen by some as an indication of the public's lack of confidence in medicine's ability to control pain in terminal patients Physicians speaking against the initiative admitted that pain management was often inadequate, and claimed if pain was alleviated, there would be no need for proposals to decriminalize doctor-assisted dying.

With the state Hemlock Society chapter as the nucleus and catalyst, the coalition put forward a campaign which set new standards for fundraising in Washington. Initiative supporters raised over $1.6 million from some 27,000 individual contributors nationwide. Phone solicitors made follow up calls to direct mail recipients, and while the phoning may have displeased some persons, the total amount raised far outpaced other grassroots campaigns.

Most of the funds raised against 119 came directly or indirectly from the bishops of the Roman Catholic Church, either through Thomas Murphy, the Archbishop of Seattle, or the National conference of Catholic Bishops in Washington, DC. Groups like the Knights of Columbus also pledged hundreds of thousands of dollars, and funds were collected at parish churches across the state.

Physicians in Washington were divided about the aid-in-dying proposal. One group, Physicians for YES on 119, brought Dr. Timothy Quill from Rochester, New York, to Seattle for press conferences in favor of physician assistance to patients seeking to die. The group reports that its members in active practice have noted no ill effects on their businesses, and have, in fact, gained new patients seeking out doctors who supported 119.

The Medical Association leaders, on the other hand, became increasingly alarmed when it looked like the initiative would pass. They based their message on the theme that doctors could not be trusted to implement a euthanasia law in a responsible manner. They predicted that unprincipled doctors would ignore the safeguards in the new law and kill patients who were not even terminal without the patient's request or consent.

"Catholics rejoice in 119 defeat." ***Chicago Tribune*****, November 12, 1991.**

The *Chicago Tribune* article referred to above closes with Bishop John Nevins of Venice, Florida, asking Archbishop Tom Murphy of Seattle for advice on strategies for dealing with euthanasia supporters. "A first step," Murphy said, "is to discourage suicide to relieve pain, and remind older people particularly of 'the redemptive value of human suffering.'"

In the week before the vote, Dr. C. Everett Koop appeared on anti-119 commercials. Known for his work during the Reagan years in opposing smoking and hysteria about AIDS, many voters were unaware that Koop has long stated that his Christian faith makes him opposed to any form of euthanasia. When he appeared on Washington television asserting that voters should not overturn "a two-thousand year old tradition against killing," many voters were persuaded to desert the initiative.

As the campaign to legalize euthanasia opens in California, it is being led by the two attorneys who in 1986 drew up the original legislation—Robert Risley and Michael White. They have remained faithful to the principle that, while physician assisted suicide is a basic right, it must be surrounded with safeguards against abuse.

Initiative provisions. The California Death With

Dignity Act provides for physician aid-in-dying for terminally ill, competent adults. The safeguards that were written into the earlier 1988 act (the Humane and Dignified Death Act) remain, requiring that the decision to request aid-in-dying be in writing and witnessed by two disinterested persons; the determination of a terminal condition be made by two physicians who have examined the patient; the request must be a voluntary act of the patient; physicians who do not wish to participate are free to refuse to do so; insurance policies are not affected; and perhaps most importantly, physicians who provide aid-in-dying are protected from criminal, civil or administrative liability.

The Initiative would permit only a licensed physician to assist the dying person.

Patient control. The issue this Initiative addresses is really one of control by the individual patient. Patients facing terminal illness, loss of control of life, and the end of quality in their lives should be permitted the compassionate assistance of a physician who can help to end a life with dignity.

Lives will be extended if patients have certainty that when they determine life should end, a physician will assist them. An example of this is the early demise of Janet Adkins, who in the first stages of Alzheimer's disease, turned to Dr. Jack Kevorkian to assist in her suicide. If she had known that it would be lawful for a physician to assist her death, she might have chosen to remain alive for a longer time.

The proposed California law calls for the request to die to be "enduring"—meaning persistent and consistent. The family has to be informed of the request to die, but can neither promote nor veto it.

A physician who is asked to end a life but is doubtful about the patient's mental state can call for a psychological evaluation. The law would also require the physician to inform the state health agency of the euthanasia because such actions must always be monitored and possible abuse prevented.

• • •

Assisted suicide by both family members and physicians is already occurring extensively in secret. Why else would my book, *Final Exit*, sell more than half a million copies?

Now is the time to bring this practice under lawful regulation and public scrutiny. The euthanasia movement has succeeded in making its case through compassion and logic; now it must present the world with sophisticated legislative ideas acceptable to both the public and the medical and legal professions.

INITIATIVE 119:
Death with dignity
Washington State
November 5, 1991

"Shall adult patients who are in a medically terminal condition be permitted to request and receive aid-in-dying?"

YES: 701,818 (46%)

NO: 811,104 (54%)

Voter turn-out: 66%

Chapter 3

Personal Reactions to *Final Exit*

With the 1991 publication of my book, *FINAL EXIT: Practicalities of self-deliverance and assisted suicide for the dying*, I began to receive even more correspondence than usual. Scores of letters poured in. Mostly they came from people wanting even more information about drugs, especially those which they already possessed but were unsure about their lethality. Many were letters of thanks for supplying a book of this nature, and quite a few related stories about the deaths of loved ones. Here are two from people whose family used the book to self-deliver.

Thank you

I am writing to thank you for my mother's being able to have the death she wanted. Using your drug dosage table in *Final Exit* she liberated herself from Alzheimer's disease. She had been planning this since last October.

Thank you for your courage to speak out.

—B.B
New Jersey

Double Final Exit

My parents ended their lives together on April 11. The method which they used was one described in *Final Exit*—sleeping medication and plastic bags. It proved to be most effective and painless when done in accordance with the directions as provided.

My father was in an advanced state of Parkinson's disease and my mother had general poor health. She did not want to be left behind without her husband. Both were in the mid-seventies. Although the loss was expected, the reality was still most shocking. I do not believe that one can ever be adequately emotionally prepared; but the planning which was done, and the discussions which occurred were most helpful.

For what it is worth, we thank you for providing accurate information and advice.

—T.L.B.
Pensacola, FL

Chapter 4

AIDS and Euthanasia

When I spoke to meetings of the Hemlock Society in the early 1980s, my usual audience comprised gray-haired, elderly women. Occasionally a dark-haired woman, rarely a man. Then the audiences began to change about 1985, when the full force of the AIDS epidemic began to hit. Younger people started to come to meetings to hear me talk about ways to cope with unbearable terminal illness, and before long there were nearly as many men attending as women. The AIDS epidemic tragically brought it home to the younger generations that they could die of a terminal illness as well as their elders.

Men telephoned me to relate that they had AIDS, wanting to know about the option of self-deliverance later on. I advised them to ask their doctors for a prescription for lethal drugs, and then I would ask them to keep in touch with me. I was surprised by how often they called back to say that the doctor had written the prescription. People with other terminal illnesses rarely gave me such positive news about their negotiations with doctors for drugs.

Why were doctors more willing to help AIDS victims than other dying people? The answer seems to lie with three factors:

1. There being no cure, the AIDS patient is bound to die, perhaps with considerable distress.

2. Being gay and "out of the closet," he would be less likely to have close family who would kick up a fuss about an accelerated death.

3. From his lifestyle, his dress, and his homosexuality, it was easily discernible that he was independent-minded, and the doctor would not fear repercussion.

Of course, we are talking here of physician-aided death only through the giving of a prescription for a lethal amount of powerful barbiturates, not death by injection. When the self-deliverance by the prescription eventually takes place—if in fact in does—the doctor is nowhere near. (At present, it is still a crime for a doctor to write a prescription knowing that it will be used for suicide.) Anyway, nurses, clergymen and families tell me that a doctor is very rarely at the deathbed of any dying person.

Nowadays, many persons with AIDS have what are

called "direct lines" permanently attached to their bodies, connected to a vein, for the constant infusion of therapeutic medicines. Sometimes the patient uses the direct line to self-administer lethal drugs in liquid form.

In cities like San Francisco and Los Angeles there are underground support groups for AIDS victims who want to commit suicide at a certain point. (The act of suicide itself is not a crime, but assistance is.) Such groups supply the drugs from street sources, and if the AIDS sufferer has no companion to sit with them as they die, a volunteer provides the necessary company.

One group which acted openly in the assisted suicide of gay persons was "Safe Passages," operating chiefly in west Los Angeles. Marty James, its founder, defied the law and the taboo by going on the television programs "Nightline" and "60 Minutes" to tell in graphic detail how he had helped people to die. After the "Nightline" appearance a pro-life organization brought a criminal complaint against Marty, and the Los Angeles district attorney had to open an inquiry. Marty surrendered to the police accompanied by an attorney, Michael White, of Encino, California, provided by the Hemlock Society, and made a clean breast of his actions.

Despite his confession, no criminal charges followed because, as the district attorney explained, there was only Marty's word that he had committed crimes, and a person cannot be convicted on his own statements alone. Later, when the reporter on "60 Minutes" was pressing

Marty hard about his actions, trying to get him to express regrets or admit to a guilty conscience, the young man stood his ground, saying that his actions were not only common compassion but necessary in today's world. Closing the program, the reporter asked a final question: "What should we do instead?" Marty fired back unhesitatingly: "Change the law."

Marty, who had had AIDS for four years, died by his own hand on Christmas Day, 1991. His lover was with him. Over a five-year period Marty had helped fourteen persons with AIDS to die. They could not wait for the law to be changed.

How much assisted suicide is being practiced in the gay communities of America, illegally and covertly? No one knows for sure. It is not something about which statistics are kept. But from what I hear from different sources, my guess is that perhaps as many as half the AIDS deaths are from self-deliverance or assisted suicide. I hear of cases where the sick person lets it be known in his social circle that he intends to die at a certain time so that close friends may gather at the house that day to say their goodbyes and to show solidarity. The only person who should be there and is not is the doctor. Who can blame him? Until the law is changed, he has too much to lose.

Chapter 5

The Ethicist

You must have noticed in the newspapers and on television that we have bred a new profession—the ethicist. Everywhere they make sweeping judgments about the quality of our lives, advise us how we ought to think. Their favorite phrase is, "It's not good public policy."

Hospitals often employ them to help doctors with difficult moral decisions. That is not a bad idea as far as it goes, but through their volumes of learned papers and now the media, these ethicists are attempting to become the arbiters of our social values.

The are born out of various branches of academia. They are not quite up to calling themselves philosophers or moralists, perhaps for lack of the courage of their convictions. "Ethicist" is a title that anyone can take; it is the proliferating, trendy profession of the 1990s.

I have a vested interest here. The bulk of this nation's scores of so-called ethicists are against euthanasia, which I support. The basis of their opposition appears to lie in ancient history (the Hippocratic oath, for instance) and an ingrained fear of breaking tradition.

Reformers they are not. While they come over on television as seemingly independent voices, their salaries are invariably paid by institutions that reflexively support the status quo.

Their favorite catchphrase is that euthanasia "would not be good public policy," but I have caught a few out by asking what they will want when they face their own terminal illnesses. They want the option to check out.

These junior philosophers, from my observation as executive director of a large patients' rights organization, seem to cut little ice with the general public. Ethicists offer warnings and theories—never answers.

What the public is looking for after two decades of debate on the right-to-die issue is solutions. The medical establishment has let the people down by keeping its eyes fixed on the ethics of Greece 2,000 years ago, ethics that were appropriate for the age.

Our legislators are so intimidated by the right-to-life movement that they will not confront reform of laws governing assistance in dying. As courts that struggle with the cases of those accused of aiding compassionate death keep reminding lawmakers, they bear the onus for reform.

So, here again, the public is taking the law into its own hands. Initiative 119 in Washington state, on the ballot Nov. 5, will decide whether the voters want lawful physician-assisted suicide for the dying. This is the first such widespread test of public opinion.[1]

This fall, a group called Californians Against Human Suffering will collect signatures to qualify a similar state initiative. Opinion polls indicate likely victory in both states.

I have not seen one ethicist, one of these instant philosophers, come out firmly on the side of these initiatives, an indicator of their ivory-towered separation from public opinion. Instead they indulge in sweeping statements about no doctor wanting the option of being able to administer voluntary euthanasia. In fact, quite a few doctors will welcome the freedom from risk of prosecution that reform of the law would bring.

Instead of pontificating from TV studios, ethicists should be doing field research in hospitals and nursing homes and among the people. Those few ethicists who already favor reform should speak out more boldly, before their newborn profession becomes known as the mouthpiece of the status quo.

NOTE

1. The Initiative failed, 54 percent to 46.

Chapter 6

Euthanasia: Is It Mercy or Murder?

When active voluntary euthanasia becomes lawful—which it certainly will in many countries within the next five to ten years—it is not something every dying person will want or need. Yet getting legal help with a dying process unbearable to the patient will be a comfort to a good many sufferers, and will relieve prosecution worries for those physicians who today perform the act covertly.

Moreover, legalizing the right to choose to die will have two additional benefits: First, it will provide comforting assurance to those who would want this right in the future if they were suffering. Countless thousands, even though they would prefer a doctor's help, have stored or wish to store lethal amounts of drugs because they fear a bad death.

Second, legalization will lengthen the life for many. From my position as executive director of the Hemlock Society, I observe numerous suicides of people who, lacking such legal means, end their lives early because they fear the loss of control later on.

People often ask me how I came into this rather unusual movement and how I've lasted twelve years. I had no knowledge or interest in euthanasia until one day my first wife, Jean, asked me to help her die. She was suffering from breast cancer that had metastasized into her bones. She and I both knew her death was only a matter of time.

I saw the logic of her request and agreed to secure a lethal potion of drugs with which she could end her life at a time chosen by her. She was insistent that she would pick the time; in fact, she had a remission and hung on for a further nine months.

But in March 1975, when she was critically ill and very debilitated, her doctors gently informed her that there was nothing left they could do. Jean discharged herself from the hospital, and three days later asked me for the drugs. After we had spent several hours saying our last goodbyes, she drank a cup of coffee containing the drugs—which a sympathetic doctor illicitly had supplied—and died peacefully.

Without fully realizing the consequences, I published a little book called *Jean's Way*, in 1978. The book's worldwide publication, plus the ensuing debate that it triggered, made me a well-known proponent of euthanasia. I knew my action in helping Jean die was illegal, but fortunately, the London public prosecutor who had ordered an inquiry when the book appeared, realized from the evidence that Jean was the prime mover in her suicide. I was not prosecuted.

Even after I moved to the United States and became a writer for the *Los Angeles Times,* the subject of euthanasia would not go away. People kept asking me to do something about it. In Britain and the United States, suicide and attempted suicide are no longer crimes, but assisted suicide still is everywhere. So in 1980, I formed the Hemlock Society to educate the public through books, newsletters, and public speeches, and to set the scene for the legal reform on euthanasia that is going to be a major battleground in the 1990s. As with abortion rights, the right to choose to die is a so-called "pro-choice" controversy. Abortion and the right to die differ in that the mother is deciding for the unborn fetus, while in euthanasia, individuals decide for themselves—a much stronger argument.

A law such as the *Death With Dignity Act,* now being proposed in the state of Washington, would decriminalize assisted suicide, but only in the case of a dying person who made a written request, and provided it was willingly carried out by a physician.

If the Washington campaign succeeds (the first such campaign in California in 1988 failed through weak organization) physician-assisted aid-in-dying could be law there by 1992. The states of Oregon, Florida, and California are planning euthanasia legalization campaigns during the same period. The Netherlands is the only country in the world that has given the green light to euthanasia. Since a 1984 Dutch Supreme Court case, physicians there are allowed to give a lethal injection to a dying patient who makes a clear and consistent request.

Most politicians are leery of this issue at present, and members of the Dutch parliament are no exception. It is still a crime when a physician in the Netherlands helps a person to die, but the physician need not fear prosecution so long as the criteria laid down by the Supreme Court are followed.

In Britain, where the euthanasia society now called EXIT was founded back in 1935, a supportive parliamentary lobby is building, and a sixth legislative attempt is not far off. Across the world, thirty societies in twenty countries promote the idea of lawful assisted suicide for the dying. There are four societies in Australia, two in Belgium, one in Spain and one group in India.

In the twelve years I have been involved in this cause, I find two principal reasons for euthanasia that are constantly evidenced by polls in numerous countries:

One. Public dread of dying while connected to sophisticated life-support equipment, which creates loss of personal control over one's life, a drain on family finances, or both.

Two. People demanding the choice to make up their own minds because easily understandable public information on medical matters is now readily available in print, on radio, and on television.

Why, some ask, is euthanasia necessary when good pain management through careful use of drugs is available to almost everybody in developed countries? I have listened to many medical voices on pain control, and they summarize the situation as being able to control the pain of terminal illness in about 90 percent of cases. This means that if you take the statistic that three thousand people die every day in the United States, then about three hundred people meet their end while suffering. Also, what makes one person's life happy and bearable is different from another's. Inability to read would be unendurable to some, but inconsequential to others, and so on. Then there are the factors of distress, personal indignities, and the psychic pain of death. Loss of bowel control, indigestion, itching, and numerous other disorders may be minor to the physician, but excruciating to the patient.

In the United States, the debate on the right to die has reached all the way to the Supreme Court for the first time. The parents of Nancy Cruzan, whose brain was damaged severely in a car accident seven years ago, are seeking permission to have their daughter disconnected from her life-support system. If permission is granted as this article goes to press, the tubes that supply her with nutrition and hydration will be disconnected, and over the next few weeks she will starve to death.

With cases like Nancy Cruzan's, we are talking about what is known as "passive euthanasia"—allowing someone to die by disconnecting life-support equipment. If Nancy had signed a Living Will, she could have been allowed to die within a few months of her car accident because, in effect, she would have signed a "release."

Forty states[1] of the United States have legalized Living Wills, and millions of Americans have signed them. There is another useful document available under U.S. law—the Durable Power of Attorney for Health Care. With this piece of paper, you can assign someone else to make medical decisions for you should you become incompetent. This authority can include disconnection of life-support equipment, but it does not include permission to actively end your life.

The Hemlock Society recommends that everybody sign these documents to protect themselves to the fullest extent the law allows, but also feels that there should be another form of escape from suffering available: active voluntary euthanasia—helping a patient to die through physician-assisted suicide.

Until this becomes law (as outlined at the start of this

article), people who want release from terminal suffering must practice what is known as "self-deliverance." To assist in doing this properly, Hemlock has for nine years published a book, *Let Me Die Before I Wake*. The book gives instructions on how to end one's own life, including a section telling how not to get loved ones into legal trouble.[2]

But Hemlock looks forward to the day when it can scrap its suicide manual. We hope patients will have access to lawful aid-in-dying from physicians, on very clearly defined terms, and with appropriate safeguards against abuse. For me and many others, the right to die in a manner of one's own choosing is the ultimate civil liberty.

Notes

1. Forty-four states by the end of 1991.
2. In 1991 Hemlock published a companion book to *Let Me Die Before I Wake* entitled *Final Exit: The Practicalities of Self-Deliverance and Assisted Suicide for the Dying.*

Chapter 7

The Case for Rational Suicide

Is it a sin to rush into the secret house of death ere death dare come upon us?

—Shakespeare

The Hemlock Society is dedicated to the view that there are at least two forms of suicide. One is emotional suicide, or irrational self murder in all its complexities. Let me emphasize that the Hemlock Society view on that form of suicide is approximately the same as the American Association of Suicidology, and the rest of society, which is to prevent it where you can. We do not encourage any form of suicide for mental health or unhappy reasons.

But we say that there is a second form of suicide: justifiable suicide. That is, rational and planned self-deliverance. Put another way, this is autoeuthanasia, using suicide as the means. I don't think the word "suicide" really sits well in this context, but we are stuck with it.

What the Hemlock Society and its supporters are talking about is autoeuthanasia. But we also have to face up to the fact it is called suicide by the law. (Suicide is not a crime in the English-speaking world, neither is attempted suicide, but assistance in suicide for any reason remains a crime. Even if the person is requesting it on the grounds of compassion and the helper is acting for the best of motives, it remains a crime.)

The word "euthanasia" comes from the Greek—*eu* good and *thanatos* death. But there has been a more complex meaning developed in recent times. The word euthanasia has now come to mean doing something about achieving a good death. Doing something, either positive or negative, about getting that good death.

Suicide can be justified ethically by the average Hemlock Society supporter for the following reasons:

One. Advanced terminal illness which is causing unbearable suffering to that individual. This is the most common reason for self-deliverance.

Two. Grave physical handicap which is so restricting that the individual cannot, even after due consideration and training, tolerate such a limited existence. This is fairly rare as a reason for suicide, despite the publicity surrounding Mrs. Elizabeth Bouvia's court cases.

What are the ethical parameters for autoeuthanasia?

A) *Being a mature adult.* That is essential. The exact age will depend on the individual.

B) *That it is clearly a considered decision.* You have to indicate this by such direct ways as belonging to a right to die society, signing a Living Will, signing a Durable Power of Attorney for Health Care. These documents do not give anybody freedom from criminality in assistance in suicide but they do indicate clearly, and in an authoritative way, what your intention was, and especially that this was not a hasty act.

C) *That the self-deliverance is not made at the first knowledge of the life-threatening illness and that reasonable medical help is sought.* We certainly do not believe in giving up the minute that you are informed that you are terminal, which is a common misconception of critics.

D) *That the treating physician has been informed and his response taken into account.* What his response will be depends on the circumstances of course, but we advise our members that as autoeuthanasia (or rational suicide) is not a crime there is nothing a doctor can do about it. But it is best to inform him and hear his response. You might well be mistaken—perhaps you misheard or misunderstood the diagnosis. Usually you will meet a discreet silence.

E) *Have made a will disposing of your worldly effects.* This shows evidence of a tidy mind and an orderly life; again, something which is paramount in rational suicide.

F) *Make plans to exit this life which do not involve others in criminal liability.* As I mentioned earlier, assistance in suicide is a crime, albeit a rarely punished crime, and certainly the most compassionate of all crimes. Very few cases ever come before the courts, perhaps one every four or five years in each of Britain, Canada, and America.

G) *Leave a note saying exactly why you are self-destructing.* Also, as an act of politeness, if the act of self-destruction is done in a hotel, leave a note of apology to the staff for inconvenience and embarrassment caused. Some people, because of the criminality of assistance in suicide, don't want to put their loved ones through any risk, will leave home, go down the road, check into a hotel and take their life.

Many autoeuthanasia cases through the use of drugs go absolutely undetected by the doctors. Especially now when autopsies in this country have become the exception rather than the rule. Autopsies are performed on only 12 percent of patients today compared to 50 percent in 1965[1] because of high cost, the pointlessness of most autopsies and also, of course, autopsies often catch doctors' misdiagnosis. One study showed 29 percent of death certificates did not correlate to the autopsy finding.[2] Many doctors these days are preferring not to have an autopsy unless there is good scientific reason or foul play is suspected.

We in the Hemlock Society find that police, paramedics and coroners put a very low priority on investigation of suicide when evidence comes before them that the person was dying anyway. Detectives and coroners' officers will walk away from the scene immediately after they are satisfied that the person who has suicided was terminal.

But, having considered the logic in favor of auto-euthanasia, the person should also address the countervailing arguments:

Should the person instead go into a hospice? Put bluntly, hospice makes the best of a bad job and they do so with great skill and love. The euthanasia movement supports their work. But not everyone wants a beneficent lingering; not everyone wants that form of treatment and care. Hospice cannot make dying into a beautiful experience although they do try hard. At best hospice is really appropriate medicine and care, which everybody deserves. A major study has recently shown that most hospitals have adopted hospice standards, so hospice has done a marvelous educative job.[3] We do not feel there is any cross purpose between euthanasia and hospice; both are appropriate to different people, with different values.

The other consideration is the question: does suffering ennoble? Is suffering a part of life and a preparation for death? Our response here is that if that is your firm belief then you are not a candidate for voluntary euthanasia. It is not an option ethically.

But we should remember that in America there are millions of agnostics and atheists and people of varying religions and denominations and they have rights too.

We know that a good 50 percent of the Hemlock Society members are strong Christians and churchgoers, and that the God they worship is a God of love and understanding. As long as their autoeuthanasia was justifiable and met the conditions of not hurting other people then they feel that their God would accept them into heaven.

Another consideration is whether, by taking your life before the illness runs its full course, you are depriving yourself a valuable period of good life, and also depriving your family and friends of your love and companionship. Here again, there is a great deal of misunderstanding about our point of view and what actually happens.

Practitioners of active voluntary euthanasia almost always wait to a late state in the dying process; some even wait too long and go into a coma and are frustrated in a self-deliverance.

For example, one man who was probably this country's greatest enthusiast for autoeuthanasia, Morgan Sibbett, had lung cancer and he not only intended at some point to take his life, but he was going to have an "education" movie made about his technique. I thought the plan was in poor taste myself, and would have nothing to do with it, but it shows the level of his enthusiasm. In any event, Morgan Sibbett died naturally. He had a strong feeling for life, and he hung on, not realizing how sick he was and suddenly passed out and died within a couple of hours. Obviously he didn't need autoeuthanasia.

My first wife told me her intention to end her life quite deliberately nine months before she actually did so. When she died by her own hand, with drugs that I had secured from a physician and brought to her, she was in a pitiful physical state and I estimate between one to three weeks from certain death.

Her doctor, by the way, when he came to see her body, assumed that she had died naturally. It was that late.

From my years since then in the Hemlock Society, hearing the feedback of hundreds, maybe thousands, of cases, I can assure you that most euthanasists do enjoy life, love living, and their feeling for the sanctity of life is as strong as anybody's. Yet they are willing to make a bargain if their dying is distressing to them to forego a few weeks of the end and leave under their own control.

What is also not generally realized in the field of euthanasia is that, for many people, just knowing how to kill themselves is in itself of great comfort and often extends lives. Once a person knows how to make his/her exit and has the means, he/she will often renegotiate the conditions of dying.

An example quite recently was a Hemlock member in his nineties who called up and told me his health was so bad he was ready to terminate his life. He ordered and purchased the latest edition of *Let Me Die Before I Wake*,[4]

Hemlock's book on how to kill yourself, and called back a week or so later to say that he had got a friend in Europe to provide him with a lethal overdose. So everything was in position.

"Where do you stand now?" I asked cautiously. "Oh, I'm not ready to go yet," he replied. Now that he had the means to make his exit, he was convinced that he could hold on longer. Thus, with the control and choice in his grasp, he had negotiated new terms concerning his fate.

Surely for those who want it this way this is commendable and is in fact an extension rather than a curtailment of life. To illustrate this, I would quote Shakespeare again, "The sense of death is most apprehension."

NOTES

1. *Philadelphia Inquirer,* November 28, 1958.
2. *Seattle Times,* November 14, 1985.
3. Robert L. Kane et al, "A Randomized Controlled Trial of Hospice Care." *The Lancet* 8382 (April 21, 1984) 891-893.
4. Available in bookstores as a Dell paperback ($10.00) or at $13.00from the Hemlock Society, P.O. Box 11830, Euguene, Oreg. 97440.

Chapter 8

Offering Euthanasia Can Be an Act of Love

The American Medical Association's decision to recognize that artificial feeding is a life-support mechanism and can be disconnected from hopelessly comatose patients is a welcome, if tardy, acceptance of the inevitable.

Courts in California and New Jersey have already ruled this way, and although a Massachusetts court recently ruled in an opposite manner, this is being appealed to a higher court.

The AMA's pronouncement is all the more welcome because it comes at a time when the benefits of some of our modern medical technologies are in danger of being ignored because of the public's fear that to be on life-support machinery can create problems.

People dread having their loved ones put on such

equipment if it means they are never likely to be removed if that proves later to be the more sensible course. As medical ethicist and lawyer George Annas has said, "People have rights, not technologies."

The argument by the pro-life lobby that food is a gift from God, no matter how it is introduced, and thus to deprive a comatose person of pipeline food is murder, is fallacious. A pipe is a manufactured item; the skill to introduce it into the body and maintain it there is a medical technology. Without the pipeline, the person would die. Food is common to all humans, but taking it through a pipeline is a technique carried out because the person has sustained an injury or suffers an illness which prevents normal feeding.

The pro-life lobby also harks back to Nazi excesses of the 1930s and '40s as part of its argument for continued pipeline feeding. True, Nazi Germany murdered about one hundred thousand Aryan Germans who were mentally or physically defective because it considered them "useless eaters," detracting from the purity of the German race.

But neither the views of the victims nor their relatives were ever sought: they were murdered en masse in secret fashion and untruths concocted to cover the crimes.

No terminally ill or comatose person was ever helped to die by the Nazis. Moreover, their barbarous killing spree took in 6 million Jews and 10 million noncombatant Russians, Slavs, and gypsies. Life was cheapened by the Nazis to an appalling degree. What connection is there between the Nazis then and the carefully considered euthanasia today of a permanently comatose person who might, as Karen Quinlan did, lie curled up for ten years without any signs of what most of us consider life?

Helping another to die in carefully considered circumstances is part of good medicine and also demonstrates a caring society that offers euthanasia to hopelessly sick persons as an act of love.

Chapter 9

Who Will Help Another to Die?

No one can truly say how they will cope with an act of voluntary euthanasia—either their own or assisting another—until they actually face the experience. But it does help to think the matter through in advance.

Some people can philosophically decide in advance that they will accelerate the end of their lives if caught in a distressing illness, and some can decide that they will, if asked, help a loved one with this act of self-deliverance.

On the other hand, some people decide in advance that they definitely will not seek euthanasia, wishing to battle it out to the end; others insist that under no circumstance could they assist another person to die, regardless of suffering and need.

In the four years since I published *Jean's Way*, telling

how I helped my own wife to die, my "confession" and the impact of the book, have induced many people to impart to me their innermost thoughts about dying. It has been my privilege to have been accorded a remarkable insight into their most private attitudes and prejudices on this sensitive subject.

The impression which remains with me is one of uncertainty as to what one will do before the emotional moment of need.

I have known those who swear they could never help their spouse die, although a rational request was made, but ultimately provided the necessary aid and comfort, having resolved their inner conflicts and witnessed the increasing pain and anguish of their loved one.

Yet there are others who positively agree to help in the self-deliverance of another and later have a change of heart.

Care for Others

There are those who decide on a carefully planned suicide to bring an end to their suffering and have the courage and determination to go through with it, even checking into a motel and taking an overdose, very privately, so that family members are not compromised legally or injured psychologically.

I have known people who have helped loved ones or close friends to die and wanted to shout their action from the rooftops, feeling strongly that the law which they broke can only be changed by their public witness. (Usually they take the advice of friends and end up being discreet.)

Some spouses insist upon sitting with their partner as they take their life with an overdose. A woman told me recently: "My husband had lung cancer for eight years, complicated with radiation side effects, and made painful by emphysema. He reached the state where every breath was agony. When he decided to end his life, I wanted to sit with him, because we had loved each other for thirty years. I have no regrets at all that I was with him at the end."

Another wife, who is a skilled nurse, told me how she had administered internally the fatal dose which killed her husband, a cancer sufferer. "We did it by agreement when he could take no more and knew that death was close," she said. "We had fought the disease together for three years; it seemed logical that the dying should be together and under our control."

It is also true that many self-proclaimed euthanasists often do not have the chance to conduct their self-deliverance (surely a more apt word in this context than suicide) because death comes to them too suddenly.

Character

It all comes down, in the end, to the character of the person and the individual circumstances of the particularly dying experience.

Conditioning factors guiding a person's attitude to voluntary euthanasia frequently are related to religious beliefs, which may be strong, moderate, or completely lacking. Whether they were brought up to regard death as an integral part of life, or taught to shun it, and whether they believe in life after death also affects them.

In some cases I have observed all these factors count for nothing: the clinching consideration is whether or not the person desiring an accelerated death, or the one asked to help, feels instinctively that it is right *for them.* This "rightness" is based on a multitude of influences, the most important being the person's life experience: A nurse is likely to be more tuned into suffering than a professional football player, to take an extreme example.

In 1974, when Jean, my first wife, asked me to help her to die it came as a surprise since we had never previously discussed the matter. It did not strike me as a shocking option in view of her condition and nature. In fact, it seemed most sensible. She had bone cancer, with secondaries, and her strong character always had demonstrated an ability to think things through calmly and to make decisions right for her.

Solo Decision

I admired three things about her approach to her self-deliverance:

One. It was not to take place until we were convinced

that no hope for further remission existed, and that no "miracle" was on the horizon;

Two. It was to be her decision alone, but to be guided by relevant information from me (such as observing whether she was acting out of depression); and

Three. She had planned her death meticulously and was wholly unashamed of her intentions.

In conversations with close friends, she would casually mention her plans.

When first the plan was put to me I recall saying, instantly and intuitively, that if our positions were reversed, and it was I who was dying, I would be asking for the same help. (Neither of us, by the way, believed in an afterlife.)

Jean lived for another nine months after we made our pact. Those were rich and wonderful times for both of us. Though her body was crumbling from carcinomatosis, she was creative, loving and purposeful with everyone, so much so that many could not believe she was dying, least of all that she knew it.

With hindsight, I now understand that it was knowledge of the exact form that death would take which gave that peace of mind. It is an old truism that it is not death but the dying that is most frightening.

Jean's home and family mirrored her life and achievements, and it was in that setting she wanted to depart. She well knew that, given the very painful illness she had contracted, her destiny, if she did not take control, would be to die in the corner of a hospital ward in the middle of the night, comatose for weeks from painkilling narcotics.

She had, after all, spent too much time in cancer wards not to have witnessed many such deaths. It was these painful observations that strengthened her resolve to seek for herself a more desirable end.

As her death approached in the spring of 1975, at the age of forty-two, I examined my conscience and the facts, as I was about to be called up for my part of the bargain. Fortunately, we enjoyed intelligent, open communication with our medical advisors about Jean's condition so there was no likelihood of a misunderstanding: she was very close to death; she had enjoyed her share of remissions, and any hope of a cure was (and still is) out of the question for her form of cancer.

Was it right to help? I reasoned that, being asked by the person I loved most, I could not refuse, even though it was a serious crime. (Suicide and attempted suicide are no longer crimes in the English-speaking world, and many other countries, but assistance with suicide still is and is sometimes punishable as murder.) I asked myself, doesn't love and long-term comradeship (we had been married twenty-two years) demand that we stand by one another in time of dire need?

On Her Terms

I could not have lived with my conscience had I refused her plea to die, nor could I bear the thought that her attempted self-deliverance might be botched.

Such a long and harrowing struggle for life (two-and-a-half years) deserved the reward of a good end on her own terms. I resolved to help, whatever the consequences.

Since *Jean's Way* was published in 1978, it has had a mixed reception. Far more women than men are able to relate to the struggle that it outlines. I believe that generally, women accept the reality of dying far more comfortably than men.

My critics—and there are many—have called me "murderer" and "killer," but I feel I did the right thing by Jean; their barbs have no effect. I am untroubled. Of course, I did not "kill" or "murder" Jean. The ordinary connotation of those words is the taking of life without permission. What I did was to assist a rational person to end a life no longer tolerable.

Obligated to Act

After Jean's death, not one of the many persons who knew of my part in it chose to inform the police. The family doctor assumed cancer was the culprit and signed the death certificate. Three years later when the book was published there was considerable controversy and the news media in Britain asked the police what they intended doing about my open confession of criminality. The police were obliged to act.

When the very gentlemanly senior detective arrived by appointment I told him I was guilty of breaking this law, fully aware that it carried with it a penalty of up to fourteen years imprisonment. I added that although I believed firmly in the rule of law (all my writings had born this out) this had been one of those rare occasions where personal, moral obligation transcended law. If prosecuted I would not contest the case, though I would argue strongly against a prison sentence.

Ultimately the public prosecutor used his statutory discretion and did not charge me with any offense. One reason, I suppose, was that the "crime" was then more than three years old and evidence would be difficult to marshal. Another reason for clemency, no doubt, was that substantial public opinion was demonstrably in favor of Jean's solution.

Of course, the police also demanded the identity of the physician who had given me the lethal drugs. I refused to divulge it and they decided not to pursue the matter further. I certainly would not risk a prosecution of this wise and humane man on account of his friendship with me.

Most people involved in a euthanasia experience have no difficulty in putting the experience behind them. Many are proud of their act of love, so I find. And, were I not at peace with myself, I could not agree to continual interviews on television and radio on the subject of Jean's death. I do not seek this exposure; media people find Jean's tale a life-celebrating event worthy of repeated publication to their public.

Chapter 10

Don't Deny Each Other the Right to Choose

Bit by bit, through court case or ethics committee, the right to die in the manner and by the means of one's own choice is being chiseled out.

The specter of an attorney at every deathbed, which seriously loomed after the cases of Karen Ann Quinlan in 1976 and William Bartling in 1985, is receding as the judges called upon to arbitrate between a patient's rights and the hospital's responsibilities increasingly rule for the patient.

With these precedents, the new ground rules for death in a high-technology society are being formed.

For instance, quadriplegic Elizabeth Bouvia has won from the highest court in California the right not to be force-fed.[1] She can choose her own time to go. The family of brain-damaged Patrick Brophy in Massachusetts was given permission to take him off life-supports and be allowed to die naturally.

The court ruling in Grand Junction, Colorado, that a severely disabled man, Hector Rodas, could starve himself to death without being tarnished with the libel of "suicide," further clarifies the murky area of whether such a death is self-deliverance or self-destruction.

Interpretation hinges on the deeper meaning of those two terms, for undoubtedly they mean different things to different people.

Self-deliverance is the terminally ill individual electing a hastened death to avoid additional suffering. If a person cannot control this crucial phase of existence, what real freedom is there in this life?

Those who still see a deliberate exit as self-destruction—or suicide—and therefore as wrong are expressing either religious or cultural taboos involving a person making a decision for which they feel only God has power. This taboo on any form of self-destruction, however strong the compassionate case made for it, is deeply ingrained as a result of centuries of prohibition both by Christianity and past government leaders.

But not all major religions frown on rational suicide. In fact, many Christian theologians are today openly arguing for a more tolerant attitude toward justifiable or understandable suicide.

The Hemlock Society argues that modern Western cultures are now sufficiently educated and socially balanced to permit legislation for accelerated death for those who request it on grounds of suffering. Present laws must be carefully modified to prevent abuse.

Many Christians do not feel that their deity is a vengeful God. Thus, if they delivered themselves from unbearable suffering, he would understand and forgive.

Whatever one's viewpoint on this prickly issue, we in the United States surely respect freedom sufficiently to allow others to make their choice.

Note

1. Elizabeth Bouvia's court victory was in 1984. In early 1992 she was still alive in a Los Angeles hospital.

Chapter 11

Helping People to Die Is the Right Thing to Do

Mercy killing is the unrequested taking of one person's life by another in order to save that person from suffering. It is a desperate act of love by a person so exhausted and unnerved that homicide laws and severe punishments become irrelevant.

Far from supporting mercy killing, the Hemlock Society tries to understand it.

We argue that there has to be a better way to handle the cases of people who want help with dying because, through illness, life has become intolerable for them.

Cases like that of Roswell Gilbert, who received twenty-five years imprisonment last week, are the tip of the iceberg in the tragedy of dying in contemporary Western civilization with its dubious benefits of longer life, higher expectations of health, and soulless and expensive medical technology.[1]

Living Will legislation so far passed by twenty-seven states[2] helps with passive euthanasia—pulling the plug on a person obviously, hopeless terminal.

This is real progress. But now we must tackle the ethical and legal frontiers of people asking for help with dying—active, voluntary euthanasia in which death is accelerated.

Hemlock believes that a mature adult ought to be able to sigh a form, "Request for Help with Dying." The essential conditions would be:

• In the judgment of two examining physicians, the patient is likely to die within approximately six months.

• The patient must have believed in euthanasia for some time and the request for death must be repeated over several weeks.

• The patient takes responsibility for the consequences even if this is a mistaken decision; the decision is revocable at any time.

• No treatment acceptable to the patient remains.

• Family have been informed and any opinion considered, but the decision remains exclusively the patient's.

• Cooperating physicians must agree both in their scientific judgment and human conscience that help with death in each case is appropriate.

• Death must be administered in a manner acceptable to the patient and within recognized medical principles—either deliberate overdose or injection—at a time chosen by the patient.

• Incurable distress is a legally insufficient basis for justification unless it is the product of terminal illness.

The Hemlock Manifesto contains these conditions in fuller and more legal details. We seek their thoughtful consideration by the public.

Notes

1. Mr. Gilbert was granted clemency in 1990 and freed after serving five years imprisonment.
2. By 1992, forty-four states had passed Living Will legislation.

Chapter 12

Mercy Denied to Roswell Gilbert

ABSTRACT: A national debate over mercy killing took place in America in the summer of 1985. The catalyst was the twenty-five-year prison sentence received by a seventy-six-year-old man, Roswell Gilbert, for shooting his terminally ill wife. He can never be paroled. Florida's governor wanted to grant the man a conditional clemency, and when his Cabinet vetoed this on the grounds that it would be a "license to kill the burdensome sick and elderly," politicians, ethicists, lawyers, and the media became engaged in a fierce controversy.

Understanding mercy killing is difficult. It flies in the face of law and order, sanctity of life, and always earns that most barbed of comments: "It is done to benefit the life-taker: to make his or her life happier at the expense of another."

Trying to comprehend mercy killing does not mean I approve of it. Surely there is a better way to end suffering? Ever since I evoked a whirlwind of praise and criticism in 1978 for admitting that I helped my first wife commit suicide at the end of a long fight with terminal cancer, I have been studying similar cases, leading to two books.[1]

My action was not a mercy killing as was Roswell Gilbert's in Fort Lauderdale, Florida, on March 4, 1985. His action classically fell into that definition by being the *unrequested* taking of another person's life in order to save that person suffering. It is a desperate act of love by a person exhausted and unnerved: homicide laws and consequent severe punishments become, for him, irrelevant.

My action (a crime for which I could have received fourteen years imprisonment) was morally and legally "an assisted suicide." Had I been taken to court—which I was not—that would have been the indictment.

My "crime" differed from Mr. Gilbert's morally in that Jean, my wife, wanted to end her life. It was her idea; she laid the plan and chose the time. I was an accessory. She lifted the cup of poison (which I had provided) out of her own free choice.

But a mercy killer does not have the benefit of mutual forethought and choice. He or she is trapped by different circumstances into believing that he must act alone.

A mercy killer takes the life of a loved one who is incompetent—unable to think or act for himself or herself. Mrs. Gilbert had spoken of wishing to die but was too ill to make a rational decision about this or anything else. Prosecution is inevitable, and it is often endured by the offender in an attempt to resolve feelings of guilt and remorse.

Peering under the layers of devotion and emotion in the Roswell Gilbert case is like reading a novel by

Dostoevski or Franz Kafka. And because it is true, it has a greater effect on our psyche.

* * * * *

Here was a couple, Emily and Roswell, married back in 1936, now in the autumn years of their lives, taking off for Spain to live the good life which they had so richly earned. After four or five years, Roswell noticed his wife becoming forgetful. She often repeated herself seconds after making a statement. There were other moments of strange confusion.

In addition, Emily suffered considerable back pain. Eventually osteoporosis was diagnosed, a decrease in the bone mass, causing bones to snap easily, provoking excruciating pain. Between 1978 and her death this year, Emily's spine shortened by two and a quarter inches due to fractures. Many other bones broke over the years. Painkilling drugs helped, but also produced side effects, particularly severe constipation.

The Gilberts abandoned life in Spain, opting for better medical care in America. They bought a condominium in Fort Lauderdale in 1978. Alzheimer's disease, a progressive neurological disorder, was also diagnosed, which caused the personality change and forgetfulness. With Alzheimer's, death comes, but usually after, five, ten or fifteen years from general weakness of the body making it susceptible to infection.

During this time, Emily became totally dependent on Roswell. She was terrified that he would die or would desert her. She could not bear him out of her sight, always running after him minutes after agreeing to stay put in the living room.

Inexorably, she deteriorated mentally and physically. "Our friends stopped coming because she was so embarrassing," Roswell later told the court.[2]

Now isolated socially, tending a demented woman with a severe physical ailment, Roswell continued to look after Emily. Everyone who knew him testified to his total devotion, even up to the moment of the killing.

"They were inseparable," said a friend, Mrs. Joy Rhodes. "Ros adored and took care of Emily. I saw her a week before her death. She'd lost weight, her hair was falling out, her walk was slow and her expression changed. I noticed that the effect on Ros was devastating. He was tired and lost. He looked in a bad condition."

Emily told Joy, her friend since 1977: "I am not long for this world. I want to die."

In their last years together, Roswell had to bathe and dress Emily, floss her teeth, and wash her soiled underwear as incontinence developed. No one ever heard him grumble.

In court, Mr. Gilbert was criticized for not having put her in a nursing home. But do they really exist for Alzheimer's patients? (Heavy drug sedation is the norm for those in nursing homes.) Particularly one so demented as Emily, who also had breaking bones? Consider the weekend before she was shot:

Emily complained of severe pains. The analgesics were not working. Her doctor hospitalized her, but she was so obstreperous she could neither be treated nor put to bed. Medication sedated her at night, but invariably, the next day, she was unmanageable and disruptive. When Mr. Gilbert realized that formal medical care was hopeless, he took her home. Although he never said so, it must have been the final blow.

He was by now unnerved and exhausted. He had had almost no sleep during the three nights before he shot Emily: one sleepless night, followed by half a night's sleep, followed by no sleep. He admits that it was then he began to think of taking her life.

On March 4 he went downstairs to a board meeting at the condominium complex, telling Emily he would soon return. Within minutes she followed him, making a scene, shouting, "I am so sick. I want to die."

Humiliated, drained, desperate, solitary, Roswell took her back to their apartment. When she was not looking, he put two bullets through her head.

Roswell Gilbert is not an emotional man, nor is he diplomatic in his language. Some remarks in the witness box could easily be misunderstood. "I was ice-cool when I shot her," he said. Perhaps he meant he was numb.

He used blunt language, such as "I terminated her

suffering" and this apparently offended some jurors. He also said: "I figured I'd done the right thing. I still do. I'd do it again if I had to. What else could I have done? The only other choice was to stick her in a nursing home, which is like a warehouse."

The prosecutor succeeded in convincing the jury that Mrs. Gilbert was not dying, although she had two terminal illnesses, Alzheimer's and osteoporosis. He made great play with the fact that she went to lunch on the day she died, was cosmetically well made-up and smartly dressed.

The forewoman of the jury of ten women and two men was quoted afterwards as saying: "She was, in fact not terminal in our opinion. She was undoubtedly in pain, uncomfortable, but somebody who could make her face up like that the day she was shot! She was not ready to die; if we felt she was ready to die, it probably would not have been first degree murder."[3]

The jury could not or would not take account of the fact that Mrs. Gilbert looked so good because her husband helped her dress, and shepherded her about in the car. It is also well known that Alzheimer's sufferers vary in condition from day to day, have tremendous mood swings, and even sometimes manage to mask their dementia by displaying the social graces previously practiced all their lives.

From talking to Roswell Gilbert privately as well as hearing his testimony, I heard a voice which perhaps only those few of us who have been tested in helping a loved one to die can recognize. Mr. Gilbert was saying, in effect, that if people have been loving companions for a great length of time, there is a fusion of minds, where one assumes the burden of the other. The suffering is mutual, as is the responsibility of one to do something about it.

Mr. Gilbert and the other mercy killers take a loved one's life as the ultimate act of love, however felonious that action may be. For them there is no alternative to action. *The rest of the world, at that point, does not exist.*

* * * * *

A man in Los Angeles who shot his sick mother told me: "When you take the life of someone you love, you take your own life. In this past year I've felt dead inside."

A woman in Arizona who suffocated her mother after a botched assisted suicide said: "I was willing to do this for her. I am not sorry I went through with it. I would do it again, even if things went wrong and she suffered horribly that last day, I probably spared her quite a long time of suffering."

Asked if she killed her mother to relieve her own suffering, this woman told me: "My motivations for doing things are never all one thing or the other. They're never all pure nor all malicious. They are always mixed."

Such is the dread of Alzheimer's disease today, that

couples who are perfectly healthy sometimes tell me that they have private pacts giving advance permission to the other partner to kill them if one gets the disease and life becomes unbearable for both.

Unless they can carry this out without detection, there is going to be an epidemic of mercy killing cases like Mr. Gilbert's.[4]

The Alzheimer's victim cannot get *voluntary* euthanasia because there is no intellectual capacity for decision making. In these special circumstances, there may have to be a family decision, in conjunction with doctors, to help the victim to die at a late stage of the disease—but only if the sufferer had firmly expressed such a wish while healthy, through a Living Will and a detailed statement.

* * * * *

In the national debate on the case triggered by the refusal of clemency, the pro and con arguments on the Gilbert case, which reflect on many other cases, were as follows:

Emily Gilbert was not dying, nor ready to die. State Attorney Hancock described her as a "well functioning human being."

Alzheimer's and osteoporosis, both terminal illness, had been diagnosed seven years earlier. Both diseases were well advanced. Prosecution evidence that she was seen out of doors fleetingly does not discount the evidence of her suffering during the rest of the twenty-four-hour cycle.

Mrs. Gilbert did not ask to die.

With her brain largely destroyed from Alzheimer's, Mrs. Gilbert could not make a legally informed and competent decision. Apart from her husband's statements that she wanted to die, corroborating evidence came from friends and neighbors of her request.

Mr.Gilbert "snuck up behind her" and shot her not once, but twice. This showed premeditation.

He never denied he intended to do it. Was it mercy-aforethought or malice-aforethought? The second bullet was fired because Mr. Gilbert was ignorant of the fact that vital signs continue in a human for some minutes after a bullet has passed through the brain. Records show that almost all mercy killers use several bullets; this has not stopped them from getting light sentences.

He should have put his wife in a nursing home.

About the only way to cope with Alzheimer's victims in a health facility is through heavy sedation. Mr. Gilbert did not want that for Emily. Her dementia took the form of excessive dependence on him. If they were separated it would have been necessary to pacify her through drugs.

He should have brought in a resident nurse.

Their apartment was not big enough. As it was, Mr. Gilbert usually slept on the sofa in the living room because his wife's pain and discomfort were too great to be able to share the same bedroom.

He should have joined a support group.

Nobody has claimed that there was one near to him. Anyway, he thought he was coping. Nobody told him he was not. Mr. and Mrs. Gilbert had always been a self-sufficient couple, comfortably off financially, and they tried to live out their lives privately.

He shot her to relieve himself of the burden of caring for her.

Mr. Gilbert *thought* he was managing all right until, in the final week, things became so bad that, through desperation, he lost his previous self-control and killed her. Anyway, he knew he was breaking the law when he acted, and would receive life imprisonment as his penalty, which can hardly be considered "relief."

If he is given clemency, then the floodgates will open and people will start shooting the dying relative for whom they are caring.

In 1920 Frank Roberts, in Michigan, received life imprisonment for aiding his wife's suicide. Since then many "mercy killers" up until the Gilbert case (fifty-three of them) have received probationary sentences. Other communities have not found a rash of carbon copy mercy killers after dealing with such offenders leniently.

According to the Scriptures, Mr. Gilbert deserved to be executed. (The born-again Christian view.)

We used to execute unhappy and unstable people who tried and failed to commit suicide. We used to imprison children for petty theft.We used to pull apart (draw and quarter) traitors. Today's more thoughtful and caring society finds better ways to treat malefactors, and "mercy killing" deserves that same tolerance and understanding, too.

Conclusion

If nothing else, the Roswell Gilbert case has fueled two important debates:

One. Is the nation spending enough time and money on its sick and elderly?

Two. Has the time arrived for lawful voluntary euthanasia?

NOTES

1. *Jean's Way* (1978) and *Let Me Die Before I Wake* (1981).
2. The author attended the jury trial as observer.
3. *Newsday.* May 5, 1985.
4. The case is now under appeal. If the appeal is rejected, Mr. Gilbert can again ask the governor for clemency.

Footnote: In 1990 Mr. Gilbert was granted clemency by Florida's governor. He had served five years in a maximum security prison.

Chapter 13

Roper Poll Shows Support for Euthanasia, and Clemency for Mercy Killer

Three out of five people in Florida believe that their governor should release Roswell Gilbert, the seventy-six-year-old man who is serving a life sentence for the mercy killing of his terminally ill wife. A poll taken by the Roper Organization at the request of the Hemlock Society shows that 61 percent of people in Gilbert's home state think that he deserves clemency, while 7 percent have mixed feelings.

The pollsters then asked those who voted against clemency if they felt it might be justified in the future. (Under Florida law, Mr. Gilbert must serve a mandatory twenty-five years without chance of parole.) Nine percent think an early release is appropriate.

While 86 percent of Floridians know something about the Gilbert case, 60 percent did not watch the television movie, *Mercy or Murder,* on January 11, 1987, starring

Robert Young, thus discounting it as a significant factor in swaying public opinion.

Sentiments among Floridians on the Gilbert case appear to parallel their feelings about voluntary euthanasia for the terminally ill. Seventy-seven percent of those questioned told the Roper pollsters that the Living Will should be made legally binding upon a doctor, with 16 percent opposed. (A Living Will is a patient's request to a physician not to maintain him or her on artificial life support machinery if they are irreversibly terminally ill.)

Whether dying people ought to be able to lawfully ask their doctor take action to help them die quicker is acceptable to 58 percent of people in Florida, with 26 percent opposed. A much larger amount of people (16 percent) are undecided on this question than on the question of Living Wills.

The Questions

One. Mr. Roswell Gilbert, a seventy-six-year-old Florida resident, was convicted in May of 1985 of murdering his wife in an act he called a mercy killing. Would you say you have read or heard a lot about the Roswell Gilbert case, or a little about it, or practically nothing at all?

A lot 52%
A little 34%

Practically nothing	13%
Don't Know	1%

Two. Mr. Gilbert claimed he shot his wife of fifty-one years because she had Alzheimer's disease and also a painful bone disorder. Furthermore, he claimed his wife said she was in pain and wanted to die. The attorney for the state of Florida said Mr. Gilbert murdered his wife in cold blood because he no longer wanted the burden of taking care of her. Mr. Gilbert has served two years of his twenty-five-year sentence. Under Florida law there is no parole for murder in the first degree. Do you think the governor of Florida should grant Mr. Gilbert clemency so that he can be released from jail or not?

Should grant clemency	61%
Should not grant clemency	22%
Mixed feelings (volunteered)	7%
Don't know	10%

Three. Do you think it would be appropriate for the governor of Florida to grant Mr. Gilbert clemency at some point in the future or not? (Asked of 28 percent of respondents who feel governor should not grant clemency or have mixed feelings.)

Grant clemency in future	9%
Not appropriate in future	14%
Don't know	5%
Not asked	72%

Four. In how many years do you think it would be appropriate for the governor to grant Mr. Gilbert clemency? (Asked of 9 percent of respondents who feel clemency should be granted in the future.)

2 to 5 years	4%
5 to 10 years	2%
10 to 15 years	1%
More than 15 years	less than 1%
Not asked	91%

Five. On January 11, NBC showed a TV movie with Robert Young playing the part of Mr. Roswell Gilbert. Did you happen to see this movie or not?

Saw movie	38%
Did not	60%
Don't know/don't remember	2%

Six. An increasing number of people these days are making out a legal document called a Living Will. This document instructs doctors to stop the use of life support machines if the person with the Living Will is terminally ill and shows no hope of recovery. There is a great deal of controversy about whether or not these Living Wills should be legally binding. Do you think a doctor should or should not be legally bound to obey a patient's request to be taken off life support machines if, in the doctor's judgment, there is no hope of recovery and the patient has signed a Living Will?

Should be legally bound 77%
Should not be legally bound 16%
Don't know 7%

Seven. There is a great deal of discussion these days about the conflict between a doctor's moral obligation to a terminally ill patient and the doctor's responsibility under the law. When a person has a painful and distressing terminal disease, do you think doctors should or should not be allowed by law to end the patient's life if there is no hope of recovery and the patient requests it?

Should be allowed by law 58%
Should not be allowed by law 26%
Don't know 16%

The poll, which was commissioned by the Hemlock Society, a national right-to-die organization based in Eugene, Oregon, was conducted by the Roper Organization by telephone with 501 people in Florida between January 20 and 23, 1987.

Chapter 14

The Trial of Dr. Peter Rosier

After ten years of struggle to get public understanding of the legal dilemma of those who must help a dying loved one commit suicide, I think we can claim the acquittal of Dr. Peter Rosier on charges of murdering his wife as a significant victory, perhaps a turning point.

The jury in St. Petersburg, Florida, on December 1, 1988, called the law an ass. Despite key factual evidence that—in purely legal terms—Dr. Rosier was guilty of trying to help his wife to die, a verdict was returned on the grounds of what I would guess were compassion and morality.

It helped enormously, of course, that the father of the dying woman, who suffocated her, escaped prosecution by getting immunity in advance. The blame was heaped on him. He didn't seem to mind, and he made no apology for having helped his daughter out of the mess caused by her husband.

The prosecution was understandably annoyed at the verdict—but they should learn to read public opinion better. Most Americans don't think this action is a crime.

What are the lessons of the Rosier trial:

• This is the first case I can find since 1920 in America that a matter of assisted suicide had been charged as murder. Was it a unique blunder by the Florida authorities, or is it a dangerous portent of things to come?

• It is time to amend the law to permit physicians to accede to written requests from dying patientsfor euthanasia.

• Juries are increasingly reluctant to send people guilty of any form of euthanasia to prison.

• That until the law is changed, people must be discreet about helping a loved one to die. Criminal charges are rare, but as the Rosier prosecution shows, you speak out at your peril.

• Don't trust a doctor to tell you how to end your life! Most don't know. (In the Netherlands it is part of medical training.)

• Meticulous planning is required for self-deliverance from a terminal illness. The Rosiers were casual and overconfident.

• Don't invite the whole family to the deliverance. In

the house where Patricia Rosier tried to die were seven other people. A physician who *might* have helped took one look around and bolted!

Botched Suicide

What happened in the Rosier household on two days in January, 1986, emerged from the stories told in the witness box at the St. Petersburg, Florida, courthouse in November, 1987.There was no serious disagreement about the facts which was why the defense attorneys took the unusual step of not calling any evidence in rebuttal.

When attorney Stanley Rosenblatt rose to present an expected lengthy defense case, he said: "Surprise, your honor! The defense rests!"

It was a daring and brilliant move. It said, in effect, that the defense did not argue with the prosecution's basic facts, but neither did it accept the interpretation of the state's attorney put on them. The jury was being called upon to bring in a moral rather than a legal verdict.

The story was as follows:

Patricia Rosier, forty-three, was suffering from cancer of the lung, brain and adrenal glands. Her physicians were agreed that she had days, at most a few weeks, to live. Her pain was under reasonable control; the worst symptoms were continuous vomiting.

Patti had heard that her death could be gruesome. No

matter whether that would be the outcome, she was the type of person who wanted personal control. Already she could see how her terminal condition was affecting her husband's mental state—he was depressed to the extent that he had already given up his medical practice at the age of forty-five. His insurance company granted him disability.

Patti told Peter that she wanted to commit suicide through an overdose of drugs. Peter said that he wished to die with her but later, at the request of their two children, agreed not to.

Patti fixed the day of her death, and arranged a "last supper" of the family and closest friends, with lobster and champagne brought in by caterers. Everybody dressed for dinner. There were toasts all around, the most poignant one being to "the Lady!"

Wanting to go out in style, and also be remembered, Patti gave away her possessions to family and friends. Patti had some time earlier appeared on Fort Myers television talking about dealing with cancer, and had agreed to be filmed shaving off her hair because of the effects of chemotherapy.

So on her last night she suggested that her husband call the TV station and ask them back for a final interview, which they did. Patti did not at that point reveal her intended suicide, only that she would be dead soon.

Family and friends all knew, or sensed, that suicide

was the chosen avenue for a woman whose intelligence, personality, and concern for others was universally admired.

After the evening together—husband, two children in their late teens, stepfather, two stepbrothers, and aunt—Patti and Peter said that they were leaving to make love for the last time. Around midnight they returned to the family room and Patti kissed everyone goodbye.

Preparing for bed, Patti vomited up her lobster and alcohol and so probably had a totally empty stomach. In the presence of her husband she took twenty Seconal washed down by a glass of water. Up to that point, of course, no possible crime had been committed.

Unfortunately, her husband, a pathologist, had not planned carefully. He had asked a colleague what was the lethal dose of Seconal and was told two grams, or twenty tablets. This is the *minimum lethal dose.*

She fell asleep. In the morning she was still alive, in a deep coma. Her husband realized he had failed her and was desperate to make amends. He could not bear the thought of her awakening after being so prepared for dying. But the other Seconal and morphine tablets in the house could not be taken by a comatose person.

He called one of the treating doctors, who came to the house, saw that Patti was alive but breathing shallowly. Peter asked him to provide sufficient liquid morphine but he refused to give more than 8 mg—a trifling amount. There was a row between the two doctors and the visiting doctor left in a hurry.

Peter Rosier got the morphine and injected it into Patti's buttocks. He made no secret of this—her brothers saw him do it. A few hours later she was still breathing and Peter went to another treating doctor and asked for help. This doctor gave a prescription for morphine suppositories, of which Peter put four into Patti.

She did not die. All the drugs combined were not lethal. (See evidence on other pages.) Everybody was distraught. Toward noon—twelve hours since the first drugs were taken—while sitting around the pool, one of Patti's brothers remarked that if he had the courage he'd go into the bedroom and smother his sister.

Shortly after, Patti's father, Vincent Delman, was heard to say, "Enough is enough." He went into the bedroom, followed by his sons, and put his hand over Patti's mouth and suffocated her. She was too far gone to resist in the slightest degree.

When the three Delmans emerged from the bedroom, Peter said, "Don't tell me what happened in there." The father and sons agreed amongst themselves not to tell anyone.

Patti was mourned, cremated, and the grieving started. The process temporarily unhinged her husband and for catharsis he began to write a book about her—a monument to Patti, some called it—entitled *The Lady*. He also tried to arrange for a television play to be done about her life.

Some twenty publishers rejected his hastily-written book and his television project floundered. For reasons that were never clear—the prosecution claimed it was to advertise his proposed book—Peter went on local television, talking to the same reporter who had twice interviewed Patti.

This was the biggest mistake of his life. He admitted on camera giving Patti something to end her life, and the state's attorney pounced, initiating an immediate criminal investigation.

During the investigation the father and brothers were interviewed but only *after* they had secured immunity from prosecution. With that safeguard they confessed to the suffocation; no charges could be pressed.

Armed chiefly with the book manuscript which told every detail except the suffocation (which Peter Rosier did not know about) and the television confession, the state's attorney started a trial on three charges: murder one, conspiracy to murder, and attempted murder.

A jury of twelve lawyers would, on the evidence, which included intent, have convicted Peter Rosier over a cup of coffee. But a brilliant defense by Susan and Stanley Rosenblatt, of Miami, poured scorn on the rightness of the prosecution, used Patti's father as "the whipping boy," made a joke out of some of the prosecution's sketchy supporting evidence. The defense reached past the law to the hearts and minds of the jury.

Deliberating for only three hours, the jury acquitted Peter Rosier on all counts. They even declined to consider five lesser counts which Judge Thompson, who appeared (as would any lawyer) to favor a conviction, had offered them.

The *Tampa Tribune* reported next day that the foreman of the jury of seven women and five men had told them: "No one at any time (during the jury pollings) said 'guilty' to any one of the charges." The jurors said they found the five-week trial emotionally and physically draining.

Elder Suicide

Interesting admissions about the amount of suicide among the terminally ill, and how the authorities deal with this, were made at the trial of Dr. Peter Rosier in Florida last November.

Dr. Wallace M. Graves, Jr., a pathologist and district medical examiner in the Fort Myers district, was being cross-examined by Mr. Stanley Rosenblatt, for the defense. A medical examiner is a public official charged with studying the reasons for deaths in his district. Dr. Graves is also a director of the National Association of Medical Examiners:

Q. In your work, Dr. Graves, you have seen hundreds of suicides, correct?

A. Yes, sir.

Q. Yet you've never had occasion to investigate a charge brought by a prosecutor of assisting a suicide; isn't that correct?

A. That is correct.

Q. And you've never seen a formal charge.

A. That is correct.

Q. ...against anyone for assisting a suicide, right?

A. Not personally, no.

Q. In your work as a medical examiner, you have learned that there are a lot of suicides among the terminally ill, correct?

A. There appear to be increasing numbers as our aging population increases and more people develop terminal diseases. We have seen—and I think it's a nationwide if not universal phenomena—more and more suicides among the elderly, particularly those who have terminal disease.

Q. Who decide for whatever reason not to let nature takes its course, but to intervene and hasten their own death by committing suicide, correct?

A. Correct.

Q. And in all those cases, or the great majority of those cases, you don't have reason to really conduct any kind of thorough investigation to find out whether perhaps a family member or a close friend or someone taking care of the person assisted them with their own suicide?

A. Well, we attempt to make as thorough an investigation as we can on any given case. But once again, the extent of our investigation will depend a lot on the circumstances, the death scene and circumstances around the death scene. Many of them are unwitnessed for example. So the extent of our investigation would vary with the individual case.

Q. Okay. But the word "investigate" gives you a great deal of discretion. Investigate can amount to making a few telephone calls, talking to a few people and then writing up a report saying in your opinion there is not sufficient information or evidence to do anything further; correct.

A. That certainly could happen, yes.

Chapter 15

Mercy at Last for Nancy Cruzan

It looks as though the seven-year-long torture of Nancy Cruzan and her family is about to end: She will be allowed to escape the living tomb in which modern medicine has incarcerated her for seven years, and at last be allowed to die by disconnection of the feeding tube.

The lawyers have had their splendid days in court; the judges have made their various and varied pronouncements over the last three years; and right-to-die groups have beaten their breasts. The Cruzan family, I feel sure, has wept buckets for their daughter.

Why do we as a society put ourselves through all this? Where is the instinctive compassion, followed by logical action, that we as civilized people owe to those who are stricken like Nancy?

Our decent response to the suffering individual like Nancy has become confused by a miasma of archaic laws, muddled ethics, headlong medical scientific progress, and, worst of all, a propensity for poking our noses into other people's business.

Nancy's parents should have been left to decide her fate after due consultation with medical staff and anybody else they respected. After all, that is what family life is about—supporting (and sometimes even thinking for) relatives so sick they cannot themselves decide.

The trouble is that we have developed such a suspicious society—fed off the largely phoney dramas on the television and cinema screens, and titillated by the exaggerated evilness of the rich and famous—that we assume there is always abuse of decision-making power. Instead, we should first assume that there is altruism in a family's intentions. The law stands ready to pounce in case of misuse.

It was preposterous of the U.S. Supreme Court last June to pontificate that without a written document such as a Living Will that Nancy could not die. How many thirty-year-olds have made right-to-die advance declarations? At that age they believe themselves immortal.

We are edging towards the time when it will be mandatory for everyone to sign such a document. It may be the only way to avoid constant litigation, to keep other people from imposing their moralities, and to husband health care resources.

Naturally, to be democratic, such advance declarations, if compulsory, would have to be much wider ranging in choices than the current ones that have a bias toward choosing death.

Perhaps the forthcoming dignified death of Nancy Cruzan will be a turning point to a higher quality debate on the entire euthanasia question—the right to be allowed to die and also the right to be helped to die. This right is replacing abortion as the issue of the 1990s.

A court in Missouri on December 14, 1990, gave permission for the disconnection of Nancy's feeding tube. On December 26, 1990, she died.

Chapter 16

Euthanasia for the Elite

In a bar the other day a man asked me if I'd heard the one about the doctor who died. When this medico arrived at the pearly gates there was a long line of people and St. Peter refused to be hurried. The physician, accustomed to VIP treatment, went to St. Peter and asked to be allowed straight into heaven but was refused on the grounds that heaven makes no distinction between doctors and ordinary mortals.

While waiting in line the physician was surprised to see a man in a white coat, with stethoscope and the inevitable message beeper, come past the line and walk straight into heaven.

"Why was he not made to wait?" exploded the doctor.

St. Peter calmly replied: "That was God himself. He enjoys playing doctor."

This joke came to mind when I read (New York *Times* and *Los Angeles Times,* November 28, 1986) that the English royal physician, Lord Dawson, had (according to historical records just uncovered) killed King George V in 1936 with a fatal dose of morphine and cocaine as the old monarch was struggling in the last phase of terminal illness.

Apparently the king had not been asked if he wanted this mercy killing but his wife and eldest son had made sounds about not wanting the old man to suffer.

Within a few months of ending the king's life, Lord Dawson opposed a pro-euthanasia bill in the House of Lords, the upper house of Britain's Parliament, arguing that it was best left to doctors to assist death whenever they felt it appropriate.

Lord Dawson and some other physicians (thankfully not all) wish to play God. For instance, Dr. Christiaan Barnard was howled down at a world euthanasia conference in France in 1984 when he said that, while he favored active voluntary euthanasia, the timing of the euthanasia should be entirely at the treating doctor's discretion. When entering a hospital, said Barnard, the patient would sign a consent to euthanasia form.

Barnard seemed surprised at the opposition he met from people who were all staunch euthanasia advocates. They wanted the patient to choose the time.

Legislation which is now being prepared in the Netherlands and in California is much more in line with modern pro-choice thinking. In both these schemes the plan is for the time and manner of death to be *negotiated* between patient and physician.

The revelations about King George's death come at a time when the medical profession is examining its attitude to the increasing public interest in death-by-request, or voluntary euthanasia. The profession is waking up to the fact that laws which are seriously going to affect their behavior may soon be on the statute books.

The conservative wing of the profession is throwing up its hands in horror ("Can we be trusted with this?"), while the supporters within its ranks usually feel obliged to keep quiet about their views. To openly back something which is at present illegal might imply that they are already practicing it. Of course, some are.

Six years of investigation into mercy killings of all shades have convinced me that euthanasia is already widely available to the elite and not just kings. Well off or well connected people often have medical friends who, in secret, will pass out lethal drugs or actually make the injection. It all depends on who you know and if the physician is willing to ignore the law.

Chapter 17

From Six to Thirty World Groups

How the modern euthanasia movement has progressed in the past fifty-five years was outlined by Derek Humphry, the world president, when opening the eighth international conference of The World Federation of Right to Die Societies in Maastricht, the Netherlands, on June 8, 1990.

He said that this congress, hosted by the Dutch Society of Voluntary Euthanasia, represented thirty euthanasia groups from nineteen nations.

The first world congress was held in Japan in 1976 with a mere six groups from four nations attending. This statistic shows more than anything the recent growth of the movement for the right to choose to die.

Some of the larger countries, like Australia or America, each have four or five groups, chiefly because of huge travelling distances. Sometimes there are two groups in one country, such as Switzerland or Belgium, because of language differences.

While some of the groups differ in their ethical and legal approach, all believe in the right of a terminally ill person to choose voluntary euthanasia at life's end.

We meet in our congresses every two years, in different parts of the world, to exchange ideas, report progress, discuss strategies, offer model laws, all concerned with the one key issue—dying with dignity.

I believe that the right to choose to die with dignity at life's end is the ultimate civil liberty for a person who has given the matter careful consideration and taken all possible steps to advise others. If we cannot die according to our personal wishes, then we are not free and democratic people.

Such thoughts and rules were plentiful in the times of the classical Greek and ancient Roman civilizations. Choice of death was then a matter of honor in certain circumstances. Over the intervening centuries, with the rise of Christianity, the issue became either taboo or obscure.

The modern euthanasia movement began in England in 1935 when luminaries such as George Bernard Shaw, H. G. Wells, and others started a Voluntary Euthanasia Society, which today is known as EXIT. The second group was started in America in 1938 by a Unitarian Minister, the Reverend Charles Potter, and is today known as the Society for the Right to Die.[1]

In the early 1970s some courageous people in the Netherlands and in Australia, perceiving the two-edged sword of modern medical technology, also began forming voluntary euthanasia societies to campaign for clearer thinking and law reform about the right to die.

But the watershed in this movement was the tragic case of Karen Ann Quinlan in 1976. This young woman was in a coma, irrevocably brain damaged, and kept alive by a respirator, artificial feeding and regular drug administration. She existed in this limbo for eight years. While the legalisms of the case applied specifically to American law, the enormous world wide publicity which the case attracted awakened a sleeping public to the need to think such matters through in advance.

The reaction to the Quinlan case in California was to pass the first Living Will law by which a person could signify their wishes not to be kept alive on artificial life support systems if their prognosis was hopeless. Since the California law took effect in 1978, forty-one[2] other American states have enacted similar Living Will laws.

Today the public is debating yet another crucial aspect of the right to die: whether it is lawful and ethical in certain conditions to help another person to die. This congress is being held in the nation which has, with great courage, humanity and legal skill, made the most progress towards lawful physician aid-in-dying. Visitors like myself hope to learn a great deal within the next few days.

To conclude, let me underline what our movement is about:

• We are definitely *not* about murder or killing or getting rid of the less fortunate people within our communities;

• Nor are we about unhappy or unbalanced people escaping this world because they cannot cope with it;

• This movement is about compassion and love for our fellow man and woman. It is about caring. These feelings alone are not enough; they must be accompanied by thought, advance planning, and perhaps new laws to ensure an individual's control and choice.

As we debate many complicated topics let us never lose sight of the main target: helping human beings to suffer less.

NOTES

1. Through a merger with Concern for Dying, the Society for the Right to Die in 1991 became Choice of Dying, Inc. It remains based in New York City.
2. By 1992, forty-four states had passed Living Will legislation. Such documents are more accurately called "advance directives dealing with medical care."

Chapter 18

Hemlock Society's Tenth Birthday

August 12, 1990, was the tenth anniversary of the founding of the Hemlock Society.

On that day in 1980, Derek Humphry and Gerald A. Larue held a press conference in Los Angeles to announce the arrival of a new group which would be dedicated to advancing in America the cause of active voluntary euthanasia as an option for the terminally ill.

Cofounders were Ann Wickett and Richard S. Scott, M.D., J.D., and there was one paid member who had joined that morning.

Asked that day by a reporter how large the Society was, Derek Humphry replied, "It's growing all the time." Next day most newspapers in America reported Hemlock's arrival. "Are you going to be in the Yellow Pages?" asked skeptical radio talk show host Michael Jackson, who was told, "Certainly."

By the end of that year there were nearly one thousand members. Today there are over 38,500 members and seventy chapters.[1] While the National Hemlock Society is a nonprofit, educational corporation, some of the chapters have a different tax status which allows them to engage in law reform activities to introduce the *Death With Dignity Act.*

From the first day of the Society's existence, Derek Humphry has been full-time staff executive director. In 1983 one clerical staff was added, and since then the staff has grown to eleven. Hemlock has branch offices in Seattle, Washington, and Sarasota, Florida.

Gerry Larue has been national president throughout, except for the period 1988–89.

One of Hemlock's strengths has been its ability to produce significant books on the right-to-die question. It has eight titles, the best-seller being *Let Me Die Before I Wake* which guides a terminally ill person in self-deliverance (autoeuthanasia). This book has sold more than one hundred thousand copies since its first edition in 1981.

Today Hemlock also produces educational video films, and has staged three national conferences and one world conference. Hemlock's staff fan out across the country on speaking engagements.

Although our detractors claim that people only join Hemlock in order to end their lives, the initial member is still alive and very much active.

Shirley Carroll O'Connor was the first person to pay her twenty dollars on the day Hemlock was announced. Then she was a noted publicity and advertising agent in Los Angeles and at the time was working on the stage play *Whose Life is It, Anyway?* when she met Humphry and Larue.

Now a widow in retirement at Leisure World, Laguna Hills, California, Mrs. O'Connor is seventy-two and enjoys excellent health. "Leisure World is a misnomer," she said. "It's one of the busiest places in the world! I'm proud to be the first member of Hemlock, watching it grow over the years."

Before the advent of Hemlock, which was Derek Humphry's idea when he measured the response to his 1979 book, *Jean's Way*, active voluntary euthanasia (also known as self-deliverance and autoeuthanasia) was a taboo subject in America. Today it is a major topic of public debate. The 1990 Roper Poll shows 63 percent of Americans support the right to choose to die.

There was an attempt by a sister group in 1988 to change the law in California to permit doctors to help terminally ill people to die ("physician aid-in-dying"). This failed through weak organization. This year and next an attempt is being made in Washington State to alter the law, and further attempts are planned for California, Oregon, and Florida.

The name 'Hemlock Society' delights many, upsets some. But it has unquestionably helped in public relations because Hemlock is nothing if not an avant garde group. The day it becomes an institution its main task will have been completed.

NOTE

1. By 1992 Hemlock had 47,000 members and 85 chapters.

Chapter 19

Questions and Answers on the Hemlock Society

When was it formed and by whom?

Hemlock was started in 1980 by Derek Humphry, a journalist and author who had emigrated from England two years earlier. In 1975 he helped his first wife, suffering from cancer, to commit suicide and later published a book on this, *Jean's Way*. Cofounders of Hemlock were Ann Wickett, Gerald A. Larue and Richard S. Scott.

Why was it started?

Because no organization in America was tackling the issue of voluntary euthanasia for the terminally ill through assisted suicide. There were many such groups in other countries.

Why call it Hemlock Society?

The root plant Hemlock was used in ancient Greece and Rome for rational suicide. Suicide, which, under certain conditions, was acceptable to those societies. The death of Socrates is the most famous example. In Western literature, the term "drink the cup of hemlock" has (through Shakespeare and others) come to mean rational suicide. This organization uses it in a symbolic fashion; to ingest hemlock is a painful and uncertain way to die.

Is Hemlock incorporated?

In 1981 Hemlock became a California nonprofit educational corporation, although since 1988 the group has operated from Eugene, Oregon. The National Hemlock Society (legal name) is a tax-exempt, tax-deductible organization classified 501(c)(3) by the IRS. Its federal tax ID number is 95-3637844. Hemlock's financial statement is published annually and available upon request along with a business envelope and fifty-two cents postage.

What does Hemlock do?

It supports the principle of a person who is terminally ill and suffering to choose to end his/her life, and if necessary get help in doing so, ideally from a physician. This is not yet lawful. Through books, newsletters, pamphlets, talks, the media, conferences, and its chapters, the matter is discussed.

Change is in the future. What if I am dying now and need help?

Hemlock publishes two unique books, *Let Me Die Before I Wake* and *Final Exit,* which tell how people may take their own lives, and how far others may go in helping without breaking the law.

Are there chapters of the Hemlock Society?

Yes. There are more than seventy across the United States and the number is increasing all the time. To find out if there is a chapter near you (a) look at page two of *Hemlock Quarterly;* or (b) check your telephone directory; or (c) call national Hemlock at 1-800-247-7421.

What do chapters do?

Chiefly it's people of like minds getting together to talk and network. There are open meetings with speakers on special subjects, videos are shown, and chapters plan fundraising or political events. Chapters have a small annual fee to defray administrative costs such as mailing and telephone.

What political goals do you have?

The ultimate aim of the Hemlock movement is to have physician aid-in-dying (active voluntary euthanasia) made lawful through the passage of the Death With Dignity Act. National Hemlock, by its construction, can have only limited political goals. Lobbying is done by the state chapters—for instance, Hemlock of

Washington State was a prime force in the coalition that qualified Initiative 119 for the ballot on November 5, 1991. Hemlock of Oregon is actively supporting legislative change in that state.

Is Hemlock connected to, or a spin-off, of another group?

No. Although the founder, Derek Humphry, emigrated from England in 1978, he did not then intend to start Hemlock, which started two years later and is entirely independent. Hemlock is nonetheless a founder member of The World Federation of Right to Die Societies, an umbrella group of thirty-one societies in nineteen nations.

Is suicide a crime?

Not any longer. Neither is attempted suicide. But assistance in suicide remains a crime, for whatever reason. Prosecutions are rare. If assistance is carried out privately, with justification, and is not publicly exposed, district attorneys are not likely to take action. But we think it would be preferable to change the law to safeguard everybody, including doctors.

Will my life insurance be canceled if I commit suicide?

Not if you have paid the premiums for two years (one year in Colorado).

Can I get personal counseling from Hemlock?

Sorry, no. There are three reasons: (a) Any one-on-one form of assistance in suicide (however humanitarian) might be considered a crime at present. (Our literature on the subject is protected by the First Amendment); (2) We do not have the requisite skills or staff to assess individual situations across the country; (3) This act is essentially private and familial.

Can I get group counseling through Hemlock?

Yes. Some chapters have weekly sessions of members only who meet to talk about painful experiences, what difficulties they are undergoing, and hopes and fears for the future. For some people, sharing feelings helps them to cope. As yet, all chapters are not able to offer support groups, but they are growing.

Are there other euthanasia societies in America?

Yes. Choice in Dying, Inc., which works only for the acceptance of passive euthanasia (allowing to die), while Hemlock works for the acceptance of both passive and active voluntary euthanasia (helping to die). The group's office is in Manhattan: 250 West Fifty-Seventh Street, New York, N.Y. 10107.

Can euthanasia be obtained in the Netherlands?

Yes, but for residents only. Since a Supreme Court decision in 1984, Dutch doctors have not been prosecuted for helping their own patients to die in certain defined circumstances. We have heard of Americans being turned away. Dutch doctors and the local voluntary euthanasia society have asked us to warn people not to come to their country expecting help which cannot be given.

Isn't England more advanced on this?

Regretfully, no. The fight to get lawful euthanasia there started in 1935, and there have been five attempts in Parliament to change the law. None have succeeded. The publicity about the fight has left some Americans with a mistaken impression of progress.

What about a book called *Exit* in England?

In 1981, the Voluntary Euthanasia Society there published a little booklet called *A Guide to Self-Deliverance*. For legal reasons peculiar to Britain, publication was stopped. Anyway, it contained no information that is not currently in Hemlock's literature, and, in fact, had a great deal less. The address of the English society is 13 Prince of Wales Terrace, Kensington, London, W8 5PG, United Kingdom.

What about a book published by the Voluntary Euthanasia Society of Scotland?

A booklet by Dr. George Mair called *How to Die With Dignity* was published in 1980 and is still sold—but only to members. Again, it does not contain anything not already in Hemlock's literature. The address of the Scottish organization is 17 Hart Street, Edinburgh, EH1, 3RO, Scotland, United Kingdom.

Wasn't there also a book published in France?

Yes. *Suicide: Mode D'Emploi* (1982). It was mainly about suicide for emotional and political reasons; it did not deal with terminal illness. Most of the information about methods of suicide was taken from Hemlock's literature. It has never been published in English. We have seen it and think it valueless for our members. It is also out of print.

Is it worth signing a Living Will?

Sure. But don't rely on it excessively. This document (legitimized by forty-four states) is a written request from patient to doctor not to be put on life-support equipment—or to be taken off it—if the patient is hopelessly ill and wants to die without further medical intervention. But note that it is a *request,* not an order. A Living Will serves most to protect a doctor against subsequent civil suit should his disconnection be disputed.

Is a Durable Power of Attorney for Health Care any better?

This is a superior legal instrument. Through it a person gives advance authorization to another person (relative or close friend by agreement) to make medical decisions for him or her if the person becomes incapable. It has the flexibility to operate in different circumstances which the Living Will lacks. A person can tell their potential surrogate their wishes and standards. It validates passive euthanasia ("plug pulling") but not active euthanasia (assisted suicide).

How do I get these documents?

Many organizations and stationers supply them. Hemlock's version is a combination of Living Will and Durable Power of Attorney for Health Care. It comes with membership or send $3 plus a SASE and fifty-two cents postage.

Do I need an attorney to fill out these documents?

You can use a lawyer if you wish but they are simple enough to complete without legal advice.

Why don't people just shoot themselves?

The credo of Hemlock is that autoeuthanasia should be nonviolent, painless, and bloodless. It ought also to be able to be aesthetic enough to be carried out in the presence of loved ones and to give them a chance to say goodbye. The discovery of the body should not be a shock. Also, we know nothing about the so-called "best ways to aim a gun," if there are in fact such best ways.

Will Hemlock give me the name of a sympathetic doctor?

We wish we could. Thankfully, there are many

physicians who believe in voluntary euthanasia where it is justified and they will in certain discreet circumstances help. However, they confine this assistance to *people whom they know* and share a rapport. We cannot supply names of doctors until physician aid-in-dying is made lawful.

Is cyanide a good means of self-deliverance from a terminal illness?

Certainly cyanide in substantial quantities is a sure way of death, but, again, we *do not* recommend it. The dying might be extremely painful. You would not want your loved ones to be present or to find you afterward.

For how long can I store drugs?

If kept sealed in their containers, in a cool, dark place, drugs will last at least five years. Even then, the deterioration is only by degrees. For every year over five, add two more pills or capsules to the dosage to compensate. A refrigerator is too damp to store drugs unless they are specially sealed. Read *Final Exit* for further details.

Where can lethal drugs be purchased?

The only method of autoeuthanasia that we recommend is through the use of certain drugs. And these, unfortunately, are all on prescription. So if a doctor will not give you a prescription for them, you will be faced with difficulties. But keep trying different doctors. Explain your philosophy.

What about Mexico as a source?

On television, both on *60 Minutes* and in a play *When the Time Comes,* the erroneous impression was given that any sort of drug can be freely purchased in Mexico. That was never true. With difficulty, Darvon can be legally purchased without prescription in a few (not all) Mexican pharmacies and sometimes pentobarbital. Purchases are hardest in the border towns, a little easier inland. Our members tell us that bringing drugs across the border is no problem so long as they are in modest quantities for personal use and have been purchased legally.

What about drugs which are lethal in overdose that you do not mention in *Final Exit, Let Me Die Before I Wake,* and the drug chart?

If a certain drug that you have, or know about, is not mentioned in these books, then it is considered from experience in the euthanasia movement to be unsatisfactory. For instance, Halcion and Dalmane are not effective by themselves, but they may help in combination with other more potent drugs. Also, if a drug is not listed on our chart, then it also is unsuitable. There are many drugs that will kill a person if taken in excess, but the dying will be slow and painful, perhaps over days, and there is then a possibility that medical intervention will revive a person. For example, to take aspirin in excess can be lethal by burning out the lining of the stomach in a protracted, painful manner.

Are there nonprescription drugs that can be used in self-deliverance?

None that will accomplish this quickly and painlessly.

Are there ways of self-deliverance other than using drugs?

Of course. But these are the ways of unhappy suicidal people who act alone and usually die violently. Hemlock favors peaceful, bloodless dying, preferably in the company of loved ones.

What about the plastic bag method?

This requires great care. The technique is explained in *Final Exit.*

Who are your main opponents?

The hierarchy of the Roman Catholic Church. Put simply, they believe that only God gives life and only He takes it away. Yet there is evidence that many lay Catholics believe in justified, lawful voluntary euthanasia. Similarly, Orthodox Jewish doctrine opposes euthanasia but many Jewish people support it. Hemlock respects these official positions, feeling that there is room for differing points of view within a free society.

Which churches support euthanasia?

The Unitarian church and the United Church of Christ have voted endorsement of the right-to-die. Most other churches leave it to personal conscience according to circumstances.

How much of the public supports euthanasia?

According to frequent polls, about 80 percent of Americans support passive and 60 percent support active euthanasia. Hemlock has approximately 67,000 members and 85 chapters. It has sold more than 150,000 copies of *Let Me Die Before I Wake.*

Won't there be abuse if voluntary euthanasia is legalized?

Our Death With Dignity Act will introduce lawful regulation which is lacking now. It contains penalties for abuse. More broadly there is nothing in life which isn't abused from time to time. Politicians are sometimes corrupt; priests are occasionally imprisoned for offenses; policemen have been known to use excessive violence. But we still rely on their institutions to hold together the fabric of society. Voluntary euthanasia will be supervised under the ordinary rule of law and administered with the human decency and compassion that most people practice.

Should I join the Hemlock Society?

Look into your conscience, ask yourself about the standards you wish when the inevitable end comes, and decide. We certainly need all the support we can get to legitimize the ultimate civil liberty: the right to choose how and when to die.

Annual membership costs $25 single and $35 for a

couple. Senior citizens over 62 may join for $15 single and $20 for a couple. Get a membership form by calling 1-800-247-7421 or writing to Hemlock at P.O. Box 11830, Eugene, or 97440-4030.

Chapter 20

Eleven Doctors Accused in USA

Eleven medical doctors have been charged with killing a terminally ill patient or family member.

None, however, has been sent to prison. The cases are:

1935

A general practitioner in Montevista, Colorado, **Harold Blazer,** was accused of the murder of his thirty-year-old daughter, Hazel, a victim of cerebral spinal meningitis. Evidence was given that she had the mind of a baby and her limbs were the size of a five-year-old child.

Dr. Blazer, together with his wife and another daughter, had taken care of Hazel for thirty years. One day he placed a handkerchief soaked in chloroform over her face and kept it in place until she died.

At his trial, the doctor was acquitted.

1950

New Hampshire doctor **Hermann N. Sanders** was charged with first degree murder of a terminally ill patient, Abbie Borroto. At the request of Borroto's husband, Sanders injected Borroto with 40 cc's of air and she died within ten minutes. When he logged the fatal injection into the hospital record, Sanders was reported to authorities.

At the close of a three week trial, the jury deliberated an hour and ten minutes before returning a verdict of innocent.

1972

Long Island doctor **Vincent Montemarano,** chief surgical resident at the Nassau County Medical Center, was indicted on a charge of willful murder in the death of fifty-nine-year-old Eugene Bauer.

Bauer, suffering with cancer of the throat, had been given two days to live. Bauer died within five minutes of Montemarano's injection of potassium chloride.

The defense argued that the state didn't prove Bauer was alive prior to the injection. The jury deliberated fifty-five minutes before returning an innocent verdict.

1981

California doctors **Robert Nedjil** and **Neil Barber** were charged with murder for discontinuing mechanical ventilation and intravenous fluids to Clarence Herbert, fifty-five.

The patient had a heart attack after surgery to correct an intestinal obstruction. Herbert stayed in a coma for three days before his condition was declared hopeless.

Following the wishes of Herbert's wife and eight children, he was taken off life-support systems but continued to breathe. Five days later the intravenous fluid was discontinued. Herbert died six days later.

In October 1983, a court of appeals dismissed the charges.

1985

Dr. John Kraai, an old-time physician from a small New York town, was charged with second degree murder in the death of his patient and friend Frederick Wagner, eighty-one.

Wagner suffered from Alzheimer's disease for five years and had gangrene of the foot.

On the morning of Wagner's death, Kraai injected three large doses of insulin into Wagner's chest. As Wagner's conditioned worsened, a nurse called the State Department of Patient Abuse. Kraai was charged with murder.

Three weeks after his arrest, Kraai killed himself with a lethal injection.

1986

New Jersey doctor **Joseph Hassman** was charged with murder in connection with the death of his mother-in-law, Esther Davis.

Davis, eighty, suffered from Alzheimer's disease. At the family's request, Hassman injected Davis with a lethal dose of Demerol.

Hassman cried several times in court during the trial. He was found guilty and sentenced to two years probation, fined $10,000 and ordered to perform four hundred hours of community service.

1987

Fort Myers doctor **Peter Rosier** was acquitted of first degree murder in the death of his wife, Patricia. Pat tried to end her life with an overdose of Seconal, but when the powerful sedative didn't take hold, Rosier began injecting her with morphine.

The morphine wasn't lethal. Rosier didn't then know it, but Pat's stepfather Vincent Delman smothered her.

1989

Dr. Donald Caraccio, thirty-three, of Troy, Michigan, was charged in Detroit with the murder of a seventy-four-year-old woman hospital patient who was terminally ill and comatose.

Dr. Caraccio gave the patient a lethal injection of potassium chloride in the presence of other medical staff.

In court, the doctor said he did it to terminate her pain and suffering. Evidence was given that he was overworked and stressed-out by the recent lengthy and painful death of his father. Accepting Dr. Caraccio's guilty plea, the judge imposed five years probation with community service.

1990

Dr. Richard Schaeffer, sixty-nine, was arrested under suspicion of having caused the death by injection at home of a patient, Melvin Seifert, seventy-five, of Redondo Beach, California, who was suffering from the effects of a stroke and other ailments.

The dead man's wife, Mary, seventy-five, was also arrested. Both were released pending further investigations, and a year later it was announced that there would be no charges.

1990

Dr. Jack Kevorkian was charged in December with the first degree murder of Hemlock Society member Janet Adkins who died on June 4. Suffering from early stage Alzheimer's disease, Mrs. Adkins flew from her home in Portland, Oregon, to Michigan, where Dr.

Kevorkian connected her to his so-called "suicide machine." She chose the time to press a button which resulted in lethal drugs entering her body. Ten days after being charged, a court dismissed the murder charge.

Chapter 21

The Death with Dignity Act (Hemlock Society Model) When Passed into Law

- Permits a competent terminally ill adult the right to request and receive physician aid-in-dying under carefully defined circumstances.
- Protects physicians from liability in carrying out a patient's request.
- Combines the concepts of Natural Death Acts and Durable Power of Attorney for Health Care laws, and makes them more usable.
- Permits a patient to appoint an attorney-in-fact to make health care decisions, including withholding and withdrawing life-support systems, and can empower the attorney-in-fact to decide about requesting aid-in-dying if the patient becomes incompetent.[1]
- Requires decision of the attorney-in-fact to be reviewed by a hospital ethics or other committee before the decision is acted upon by the physician.

• To take advantage of the law, a competent adult person must sign a Death with Dignity (DDA) directive.

• Permits revocation of a directive at any time by any means.

• Requires hospitals and other health care facilities to keep records and report to the Department of Health Services after the death of the patient and then anonymously.

• Permits a treating physician to order a psychiatric consultation, with the patient's consent, if there is any question about the patient's competence to make the request for aid-in-dying.

• Forbids aid-in-dying to any patient solely because he or she is a burden to anyone, or because the patient is incompetent or terminal and has not made out an informed and proper (DDA) directive.

• Forbids aiding, abetting, and encouraging a suicide which remains a crime under the act.

• Does not permit aid-in-dying to be administered by a loved one, family member, or stranger.

• Forbids aid-in-dying for children, incompetents, or anyone who has not voluntarily and intentionally completed and signed the properly witnessed (DDA) directive.

• Attempts to keep the decision-making process with the patient and health care provider, and out of court.

• Makes special protective provisions for patients in skilled nursing facilities.

• Permits doctors, nurses, and privately owned hospitals the right to decline a dying patient's request for aid-in-dying if they are morally or ethically opposed to such action.

Note

1. Recent law reforms in Washington and California did not include a provision that the attorney-in-fact could ask for physician aid-in-dying for a comatose patient. I believe this will have to come in due course.

Appendix

The Curious Problem of Defining Death

By Cheryl K. Smith, J.D.
Staff Attorney, the Hemlock Society

The question of when life begins is one that has been publicly debated for many years, most recently in the context of abortion. The counterpart to that concept, when life ends, has not received as much notice until recently.

For many years death was defined as the irreversible stopping of the heart. This definition was not problematic until the last quarter of a century. With modern technology, however, the human body can now be artificially maintained far beyond what was previously imaginable.

Brain Death. As a result of the problems that grew out of this approach, health care professionals and ethicists began to rethink the issue of what constitutes death. An observation of such cases indicated that when the brain irreversibly loses function, the heart also stops on its own. From here the concept of "brain death" evolved.

In 1981 a number of groups, including the American Medical Association and American Bar Association, developed the *Uniform Determination of Death Act*, a model state law. This act states that "[a]n individual who has sustained either (1) irreversible cessation of circulatory and respiratory functions, or (2) irreversible cessation of all functions of the brain, including the brain stem, is dead."

As of 1986, thirty-eight states had adopted the legal definition of brain death as compatible with the end of life even when the heart and lungs are maintained artificially. This definition is generally accepted by the medical community today. Contrary to common belief, a Living Will or Power of Attorney for Health Care are not necessary to remove life support equipment from an individual who is "brain dead."

Persistent Vegetative state. Whereas "brain death" is death of the entire brain, in many cases only the upper portion of the brain dies, leaving the brain stem intact. This is called "neocortical" or "cerebral" death.

In cerebral death, consciousness is permanently lost

due to irreversible cessation of the chemical and biological functions of the brain that are needed to support consciousness. This is known as persistent vegetative state (PVS). In this state, individuals are not considered dead because a portion of their brain continues to function. This is the condition in which Karen Ann Quinlan lived for ten years and Nancy Cruzan lived for over seven years.

An unexpected outgrowth of PVS was also related to an improvement in technology—feeding tubes could keep a person alive for decades, despite that person's inability to regain consciousness or use of the cerebral cortex.

Rethinking death. As technology advances and health dollars decline, the concept of "death" continues to be refined. A number of surveys indicate that a majority of Americans would not want to be kept on life-support equipment, including artificial feeding, if they have no chance of improving. They may reason that $200,000 per year may be too much to spend for futile treatment, they want to free the spirit trapped in the body, or that existing in that state is undignified and useless.

The difficulty in scientifically verifying whether neocortical death has absolutely occurred is becoming less problematic with new procedures such as the Positron Emission Tomography (PET), which measures blood flow in the brain. However, we still have no general agreement on what constitutes life and, therefore, when it ends. So the debate has now become centered on personhood, or "That which is so significant to man that its loss constitutes the change in the moral and legal status of the individual" (Robert Veatch).

Those most fearful of expanding the definition of death to neocortical death conjure up visions of black market organ harvesting or expect others to be bound by their concepts of what constitutes life. For the present, with the debate over whether artificially administered nutrition and hydration should be withheld from PVS patients, expansion of death to include neocortical or cerebral death is unlikely.

One commentator has suggested that individuals define for themselves what constitutes death. This can be done, in part, with a Power of Attorney for Health Care. This document allows you to record your wishes regarding medical treatment in the event you become incapable of making your wishes known. If you want to be considered dead when you have permanently lost consciousness, you may state that and types of treatments you would not want administered.

We may never know with certainty when life ends; we will almost certainly never have one hundred percent agreement on that issue in this society despite scientific advances. Individuals must determine where they stand on this important subject and plan accordingly.

The New Patient Self-Determination Act: What It Means

A new law went into effect on December 1, 1991 called the Patient Self-Determination Act (PSDA) and is the first federal law to address end-of-life decision-making.

It requires by law that all federally funded health care institutions such as Health Maintenance Organizations (HMOs), hospitals, home health agencies, skilled nursing facilities, hospice programs and Medicare and Medicaid programs must inform patients of their right to prepare advance directives for their care by these institutions—and to have their documented wishes carried out.

The PSDA specifically requires action by health care institutions in four distinct areas:

Information: Before or at admission, the patient must be informed, in writing, of his/her right under that state's law to accept or refuse particular medical treatments while he/she is competent and to make decisions about the care he/she will receive if he/she loses competence. Handouts given to the patient must include an explanation of exactly which state statutes or what case law for that particular state allows as well as a description of the institution's policy as it affects the patient's right to refuse treatment through advance directives.

Documentation: Every new patient must be asked

before or at admission if he/she has prepared a Living Will and/or a Durable Power of Attorney for Health Care. The response, and a copy of the documents, if they exist, should become a permanent part of the patient's medical record and be made known to all personnel who will be involved in the care of the patient.

Non-discrimination: Members of the health care staff are forbidden to alter in any way or to determine a patient's care on the basis of whether or not he/she has prepared a Living Will or conferred a Durable Power of Attorney on another individual.

Education: Health care facilities must provide inservice education for members of their staff and public programs for members of the community they serve on the PSDA and current right to die laws applicable in their state.

Request to Physicians

In 1992 legislators in four US states introduced Bills to permit lawful physician assisted suicide for the terminally ill. The fate of these Bills—in Maine, Iowa, Michigan and New Hampshire—is uncertain, but they were remarkable for the mere fact of being introduced by politicians, demonstrating for the first time that legislators were becoming aware of the strong public feeling on the issue.

The New Hampshire Bill asked only for the right of physicians to make out a prescription for a lethal dose of drugs which a terminal patient could self-administer. It would not allow physicians to perform euthanasia in any other circumstances.

The other three Bills sought the right of patients to end their lives either by assisted suicide or direct euthanasia.

We print below the proposed New Hampshire form which patients could choose to sign if they wanted a prescription of lethal drugs. (Please note that at the time this book went to press neither this Bill nor the other three were passed into law.)

I, ____________, being an adult, of sound mind and suffering from ____________, which has been determined to be a terminal condition by my attending physician and a consulting physician competent in the category of that condition, do hereby request my physician to prescribe medication which will permit me by self-administration of such medication to end my life in a peaceful, painless and dignified manner. I fully realize the significance of what I am asking and believe that such assistance by my physician in this most final of acts is in my best interest. I hereby absolve my physician, all other authorized persons, and any health care facility, acting in good faith in accordance with my wishes, from any civil, criminal, or administrative liability arising from their actions under this chapter. I understand the full import of this request, and I am emotionally and mentally competent to make this declaration.

Signed ____________________

State of ____________ County of ____________

We, the following witnesses, being duly sworn each declare to the notary public or justice of the peace or other official signing below as follows:

1. The declarant signed the instrument as a free and voluntary act for the purposes expressed, or expressly directed another to sign for him.
2. Each witness signed at the request of the declarant, in his presence, and in the presence of the other witness.
3. To the best of my knowledge at the time of the signing the declarant was at least 18 years of age, and

was of sane mind and under no contract or undue influence.

____________________ Witness
____________________ Witness

Sworn to and signed before me by __________, declarant, __________ and __________, witnesses, on this _____ day of ____.

____
Signature

____
Official Capacity

Sources

Chapter 2: *Hemlock Quarterly*, January 1992.
Chapter 3: *Hemlock Quarterly*, January 1992.
Chapter 6: *The Rotarian*, June 1990.
Chapter 7: *Euthanasia Review*, Fall 1986.
Chapter 8: *USA Today*, March 19, 1990.
Chapter 9: *Hemlock Quarterly*, October 1982.
Chapter 10: *USA Today*, January 29, 1987.
Chapter 11: *USA Today*, May 15, 1985.
Chapter 12: *Euthanasia Review*, Spring 1986.
Chapter 13: *Euthanasia Review*, Spring/Summer 1987.
Chapter 14: *Hemlock Quarterly*, January 1988.
Chapter 15: *USA Today*, November 1990.
Chapter 16: *Euthanasia Review*, Winter 1986.
Chapter 17: *Hemlock Quarterly*, July 1990.
Chapter 18: *Hemlock Quarterly*, July 1990.

The Gallup Poll
A Right To Die?

Do you think a person has the moral right to end his or her life under these circumstances:

	YES %	NO %	DON'T KNOW %
When the person has a disease that is incurable?	58	36	6
When the person is suffering great pain and has no hope of improvement?	66	29	5
When the person is an extremely heavy burden on his or her family?	33	61	6
When an otherwise healthy person wants to end his or her life?	16	80	4

Asked of 1,018 adult respondents on November 15–18, 1990

CASUALTIES OF AGE

Why do so many of our elders commit suicide?

An investigation by
Derek Humphry

●●●●●●

If you would like to assist the author in this ground-breaking study of the reasons why so many senior citizens choose to end their lives, or consider doing so, please write to him:

Derek Humphry
Casualties of Age
P.O. Box 10603
Eugene, OR 97440-2603

Needed are:

- Case histories
- Personal experiences
- Well-argued views for and against
- Hitherto unrevealed data